BRAVE WOMEN

Building Bridges to Transformation
A Compendium

Gathered and Written by
Ellen Duffield

*Lived by Women
all over the World*

Shadow River Ink
Box 222
Rosseau, ON   P0C 1J0
www.shadowriver.ca

Ordering Information:
Available from bravewomen.ca. Quantity sales: Special discounts may be available on quantity purchases by corporations, educational institutions, and others. For details, contact the publisher at the address above.

Orders by trade bookstores and wholesalers. Please contact Ingram:
North America - Tel: (800) 937-0152
All other areas - Tel: (615) 213-5000
or visit www.ingramcontent.com

Printed in the United States of America

Publisher's Cataloging-in-Publication data
Duffield, Ellen.
Brave women : building bridges to transformation, a compendium / by Ellen Duffield.
226 p. 21.6 x 21.6 cm.
ISBN 978-0-9947487-4-4 (Hardcover)
ISBN 978-0-9947487-6-8 (Paperback)
1. Leadership. 2. Leadership in women. 3. Social action. 4. Social change.   I. Duffield, Ellen.

First Edition

22 21 20 19 18 / 10 9 8 7 6 5 4 3 2 1

Dedicated to children seven generations from now.

GENUINE THANKS to those who have shared this journey.

BRAVE
WOMEN

BUILDING BRIDGES TO
TRANSFORMATION
A COMPENDIUM

THE COMPLEXITY, CONNECTEDNESS AND CHALLENGES of our world require people who are willing to look beyond—beyond the perspective of one culture or philosophy; beyond the problems to transformational process; beyond where we are to where we could be—and who are committed to building bridges across these chasms. Bridge Building Leaders. It turns out that many women are particularly skilled at this. However, for a wide variety of reasons, many women struggle with low confidence in leadership. This low confidence comes at a high price—personally, organizationally and globally. We need Bridge Building Leaders who are BRAVE.

BRAVE, RESILIENT, ADVOCATES, WITH VOICE AND EXPANDED PERSPECTIVE

Introduction

I REMEMBER AS A CHILD FEELING THE NEED TO BE BRAVE. A bully was flicking a wet towel at us. He was much larger than I was and was standing in the only route of retreat. As a teenager being brave meant standing up for things that mattered and I understood that this sometimes comes at a cost. As an adult there was the courage it took to co-launch an international women's leadership initiative and the backwards step of later choosing not to lead that organization citing other commitments which was really code for lack of confidence. Indeed the journey has often been circular—seeming to often land me back where I started, although perhaps with a deeper level of insight.

And the journey has not been travelled alone. As a youth worker there were countless opportunities to mentor amazing young women. I poured into them in the hopes they would go further than I had. And many of them have. Yet many of them struggled with the same external challenges and subsequent internal angst I had twenty years before. How could this be? By the next decade I was serving as a pastor, accepted within the church but often feeling the need to prove and justify myself in the broader community. It was during this season that the bottom fell out of my personal world, and the question of how to build BRAVEry in myself and others changed from an interesting side note to a life quest.

BRAVE Leadership

Back to school for the third time. A research project that spanned multiple countries and cultures. Several breakthrough insights and the discovery of disturbing trends. Conversations with real women. Wrestles with organizational realities. The realization that many leaders want to create inclusive cultures but do not know how. And, as almost all quests of consequence require, a deep journey inward followed by the opportunity to put our theories to the test.

In 2010 I was invited to become the Director of the Leadership Studio at Muskoka Woods. Little did I know the platform and laboratory this would provide for us to explore how to create environments in which men and women, young and old could thrive; or how to craft experiences that would result in transformational leaders. Starting with a blank page our team invited input from dozens of gifted people. Together we dreamed of a place that would inspire the courage, character, competencies and commitment needed to positively shape our world.

Seeking to live out what we longed for others to experience our team worked with architects trained in Narrative Design to help us tell the story. Housing the community on the startlingly beautiful shores of Lake Rosseau we invited guests to journey with us. To cross the 210-foot long suspension bridge—that serves as entrance and metaphor—and to join the dialogue about BRAVE Bridge Building Leadership. We welcome you to the conversation and begin with a story…

"A fo ben bid Bont."
Ceramic, Raku fired.
By Cal Macfarlane, Phd.

There once was a Welsh King the size of a mountain. I will tell you his tale. He had an average-sized sister named Branwen who agreed to marry the king of Ireland to unify their nations. She travelled across the sea and lived in a castle there. One day a bird flew back to Wales to alert the King that Branwen was being made to scrub the floors on her hands and knees. The King, taking this as a sign of disrespect for her as a woman and for the Welsh people, gathered up all his troops. Together the army sailed, while he walked—being too big to fit in any ship. When the Irish saw the many boats—and a man the size of a mountain—heading towards them, they were afraid. So they did what ancient soldiers did, burning their bridges to slow the advance of the enemy. The King, stepping onto Irish soil, had a choice. He could advance quickly to the castle where Branwen was being held, stepping easily over any rivers or valleys where bridges had been destroyed. But this would mean he would have to leave his troops. A great leader never leaves their team behind. So instead he chose to lay down every time they encountered a river or chasm—using his own body as a bridge over which his team could proceed. Together they accomplished their mission.

BRIDGE BUILDING
LEADERSHIP

Concluding this ancient story are these poetic Welsh words:
A fo ben, bid bont.
(Pronounced: A vo ben, bid bont.)

"The one who would be leader (chief) must be bridge."

FASCINATED BY THE SIMPLICITY and profundity of this powerful myth, I travelled to the National Archives in Aberystwyth, Wales, to explore its rich history. The hours of driving on narrow, winding roads in pouring rain were more than rewarded. Welsh-speaking archivists confirmed that this legend was part of the Mabinogion, a set of ancient stories that predate Camelot and other more familiar tales.

This story provokes many thoughtful questions. What kind of people, in an era of hero worship and *Might is Right*, understood leadership in such terms? What kind of person do I need to be, to understand it now? What kind of transformational change would occur, if more of us practiced *a fo ben, bid bont* in our communities, organizations, and nations?

Perhaps this story resonated so deeply because of my Canadian heritage. The nationhood of Canada was founded on the four pillars of Inuit, First Nations, Anglophone, and Francophone peoples. To this growing mosaic the people of the world have come. As I write this, Canada is the only Western country that numbers in the top-twenty culturally diverse nations of the world.[1] Traditionally steeped in the values of tolerance and diversity, Canadians are often brought in as international negotiators and peacekeepers; sometimes even described as Bridge Building Leaders.* Sadly tolerance—like any strength taken to an extreme—can be a weakness.

Ironically, it can lead to the very things it seeks to avoid—bullying, selfishness, divisiveness and tyranny—if all behaviours and mindsets are tolerated. And sadly this national strength has been least demonstrated within our own borders (see note).

In the physical realm, bridge building involves complex engineering and construction. In *Observations on the Rebuilding of London Bridge* we read,

> It is generally acknowledged that the construction of a commodious bridge over a wide, impetuous river is one of the noblest efforts of human genius. In no country that has made any advances in civilization has the art of bridge-building been neglected. On the contrary, it has everywhere been esteemed for its great utility and has engaged the attentive care of [humanity].[2]

In the non-physical realm it is best envisioned as a construct—with profound implications—as seen in the Welsh myth.

Bridge building is not a painless process or calling. While being a bridge is very different from being a doormat, an Arab proverb reminds us that, "those who would build bridges must be willing to be walked on."

However, there is also a high collective cost when bridge building is not practiced.

---

* *Canada, of course, is not the only country to practice bridge building. Nor is Canada consistent in bridge building, especially at home. First Peoples rights have been consistently overlooked and treaties broken in ways that seriously undermine this value. When Dutch colonists first came to Canada they were offered a treaty from the Haudenosaunee, which included the gift of a wampum belt with two stripes running its length. The stripes represented two canoes going downstream side-by-side, never interfering with yet always available to the other. There is a powerful, and as yet unrealized, value of peaceful and respectful co-existence expressed in this Two Row Wampum. Additionally, refugees have not always been greeted with the respect and welcome that Canada, at her best, might offer. Also, in spite of recent advances, a significant gender gap still exists. The idea of bridge building is both aspirational and real, and is offered here in the spirit of learning.*

Bridge Building Leadership includes the mindsets, skills, and practices needed to span diverse perspectives and provide a way to where we could be.

Bridge building offers the possibility of transformation. Bridged perspectives transform relationships. Bridges to change transform results. Bridges between old and new; east and west; those who have and those who have not; what has been and what could be. In an era when—in spite of advances in technology, medicine and education—many people feel disconnected and disillusioned, nothing could be more timely.

OR PERHAPS THE STORY of the bridge-building king resonates because I am a woman. For many women around the world, bridge building is a powerful metaphor for both our strengths and our challenges.

As part of a Women's TED Talks series, journalist and keynote speaker Hanna Rosin concluded that, "a high bridge is a better metaphor for women to consider than a glass ceiling. The way is possible but a woman must be confident that she can and should be on the bridge."[3]

This confidence does not come naturally to all women longing to see positive change. Internal and external factors combine to create challenges her male peers may not experience. The way is possible, but it is challenging. Women traversing this high bridge need the support of Bridge Building Leaders who have gone before.

Bridge Building Leaders know how to *be the bridge*, not just be on it.
Bridge Building Leaders know how to *build the bridge*, not just cross it.
Bridge Building Leaders provide a way *for others* to cross.

Bridges link ideas, people, and resources, to address the needs of our hurting world.

WHAT MAKES A BRIDGE BUILDING LEADER? She is willing to be BRAVE. She is RESILIENT and therefore willing to take measured risks. She is a woman of authentic ACTION and ADVOCACY. She is cultivating her VOICE, and constantly EXPANDING her perspective, skill set and influence. She is B.R.A.V.E. enough to build bridges wherever she goes.

A HIGH BRIDGE OR
A GLASS CEILING

A BRAVE Leader:
Be You, Bravely.

On my desk sits a tiny pewter frame that cradles the words "Be you, Bravely." A gift from a dear friend, these words remind me that it takes courage to be fully myself and it takes courage to bring my full self into my leadership, to be a bridge.

The Merriam-Webster dictionary defines Bravery as "the quality that allows someone to do things that are dangerous or frightening."

What is that quality?
And how do we gain it?

As part of a coaching exercise, I was once asked to imagine that it was twenty years in the future and I was designing a book cover for the story of my life. Reflecting for several minutes, I decided to title it *Ellen Duffield: The Story of a Woman Who Dared to Face Her Fears in Order to Follow Her Dreams.*

"I learned that courage was not the absence of fear, but the triumph over it. The brave [wo]man is not [s]he who does not feel afraid, but [s]he who conquers that fear."

NELSON MANDELA

"Be you, Bravely."
Ink on Paper.
Illustrated by Erika Henkelman,
of Water Maple Creative.

Little did I know then that fear is an epidemic among women. In fact, I wonder if there might be some truth in that title for every one of us.
Little did I know then the high cost of women's low confidence.
Little did I know then that so much could be done, or that the return on investment could be so high!

THIS BOOK IS A RESOURCE, a shared journey, and a prompt for conversation. You will be given opportunities for personal reflection and small group discussion at various points along the way. Each of these exercises, while deceptively simple, have been effective in helping women and girls discover more about who they are, what matters to them, the messages and experiences that have shaped them, and the choices they wish to make in light of these insights.

Completing these exercises (alone or with the help of a friend or leadership coach) is of course not mandatory, but they may enable deeper breakthroughs in thinking and action.

Only you know how you learn best and what margin your life currently affords. Whatever route you choose, I invite you to enter into it with a spirit of curiosity and to go to the places that are the most life giving to you. The last thing we want, or you need, is for this to become one more onerous task on an already too long to do list.

HOW TO USE
THIS BOOK

BOOK COVER
REFLECTION EXERCISE

FOLD A SHEET OF PAPER IN HALF TO CREATE YOUR OWN BOOK COVER. Imagine that it is twenty years from now and you are reflecting back on your life.

What title or image would you put on the front?
What chapters would you list inside the front cover?
Who would you list inside the back cover as inspiration for and companions on your journey?
Add fears you will have to overcome and the reasons they were worth overcoming.

Then fill the outside back cover with endorsements from peers and celebrities for the work you have done. Do not be afraid to list your most powerful heroes and heroines and to anticipate the positive things they would say about your life's work.

REFLECT / DISCUSS

The ancient Roman poet Virgil once said, "Fortune favors the brave." Do you agree or disagree? How has this mindset influenced the way people in the West think about bravery?

What stops some women from being BRAVE? The answer to this question is both universal and individual, complex and systemic. For many women, thousands of accumulated, conflicting messages—at both a personal and global level—contribute to this phenomenon. We will explore the huge loss when women are:

- Unaware of how much their voice matters – see Chapter One
- Feeling inadequate – see Chapter Two
- Overwhelmed by life, not to mention global needs – see Chapter Three
- Unsure how to begin and/or afraid of lacking credibility – see Chapter Four
- Unsure what they are best suited to or passionate about – see Chapter Five
- Not being sure how to use their voice – see Chapter Five
- Not feeling prepared for leadership – see Chapter Six
- Stuck – see Chapter Six

WHICH OF THESE LOSSES MOST RESONATE WITH YOU? Or are there others that are more relevant to you?

PERSONAL REFLECTION

Being brave is an attribute that includes, yet transcends, action. Sometimes it involves the Bravery to wait; sometimes the Bravery to accept; sometimes the Bravery to compromise; sometimes the Bravery to hold out; and sometimes the Bravery to forgive.

Indeed as Indira Ghandi, first and to-date only female Prime Minister of India, once said, "Forgiveness is a virtue of the brave."

What situation, choice or relationship challenge do you currently face that will take Bravery to navigate wisely and well?

Developing the BRAVEry to step outside our comfort zone, and the Resilience—born of hope—that enables us to get up when we fall down, prepares BRAVE leaders to Build Bridges by inspiring both Advocacy and Action. These Bridges are strengthened as we cultivate our Voice and Expand our skills, perspective and influence. Before exploring each concept in this organizing acronym we delve into the reasons this work is worth doing: the high cost of the alternative.

The High Cost of Low Confidence

"Girls' self-esteem peaks when they are nine years old, then takes a nose dive," writes clinical psychologist Robin F. Goodman of the New York University Child Study Center.

According to the Center, self esteem drops in the pre-teen years because there is "a shift in focus—the body becomes an all consuming passion and barometer of worth."[4]

When I first read this startling number I couldn't help but think of the precocious 3-9 year old girls and the intelligent, competent women that I knew who were struggling with self-esteem. I wanted to know what happens in between and what could be done to reverse this disturbing trend. Along the way, I have learned that while confidence[5] can be built up again, it takes intentionality, and that low self-confidence is a significant issue for many women.

Did you catch that? Nine years old.

Indeed, a 2015 research project of female leaders in the US found that 67% of participants said that they need more support building confidence to feel like they could be leaders.[6]

THE SOURCE OF LOW
CONFIDENCE (CONT'D)

Joanna Barsh, author of *How Remarkable Women Lead,* was asked what the most common obstacle the highly successful businesswomen in her study had to overcome? She answered, "More than 60 per cent of the women said they didn't naturally have the confidence to speak up for themselves early in their career."[7]

It is significant to note that these studies were carried out among highly successful women.

I REMEMBER THE DAY THIS REALITY HIT HOME FOR ME. I was meeting with a small group of very accomplished young women. A well educated, beautiful, and articulate young woman whom we will call Mary, was also a gifted athlete competing at national levels, yet she balked at the suggestion that she was a leader. I was stunned. Having watched Mary lead in formal and informal settings and seeing the influence she had amongst her peers I would have assumed she viewed herself at such. In that moment, the implications became glaring. If this talented, bright, well-loved young woman was struggling with confidence what must be going on for other women. Only later did I learn that bright women are more likely to struggle with low self-esteem[8] and that most believe this is, "a personal weakness not a general trait of the out-of-power, and even of very senior women. They are not yet convinced that they deserve all the opportunities open to them."[9]

Only later did I learn that bright women are more likely to struggle with low self-esteem.

WHERE DOES THIS LOW CONFIDENCE COME FROM? The reasons are multi-faceted and complex. Many women express the feeling that the deck is stacked against them and the research offers compelling justification for this mindset. "[M]ost women who make it… have stories of the farcical attitudes they faced not so long ago… Many of the more obvious barriers have now been dismantled. What women are working on are [the] more deep seated and harder to eradicate issues below the surface—both in themselves and others."[10] If we could zoom out to look at this issue, we could see just how widespread and systemic it is. How massive the personal and global implications are.

It starts early for many women. A study of 4,000 American children, by the Girl Scout Research Institute, found that the greatest single barrier to leadership reported by girls was a lack of self-confidence in their own skills and competencies.[11] Interestingly, the study also showed that girls were much more likely than boys to be aware of gender biases for women leaders and tended to set much higher standards for what it takes to be a leader today.[12] These findings are significant, considering the same studies indicated that girls believe three qualities are needed to be a good leader: a positive attitude (86%), the ability to listen (85%), and confidence (85%).[13]

Not long after my formal study of this issue began, I was given the chance to meet and work with an amazing group of young women. I tried to keep an open mind. Maybe these girls would not follow the patterns suggested in these North American studies. With their smiling faces and goofy behavior, they looked at ease with themselves and each other. Yet, as soon as the conversation turned to leadership, girl after girl—chosen for this program because of their demonstrated leadership, maturity, and behavior—self-identified as a non-leader. Intrigued, I began to ask questions. The conversation soon turned to the high expectations leaders face and the tension between leadership and friendship.

Certainly not all families or cultures are the same regarding this issue. A 2013 report found that girls who identify as African-American and Latina are more likely to have leadership aspirations than Caucasian girls.[14] Latina mothers are also much more likely to encourage their daughters to speak up and to lead.[15] A similar study of eighth-grade students from around the US, found that girls who identified as African-American have higher levels of self-esteem than either African-American boys or Caucasian girls.[16] This is significant. The belief that one is or can be a leader is planted in childhood. Yet, many girls are surrounded by messages and models that distort their ability to discover and live into who they are. As a result they are living at a fraction of their capacity, influence, and true beauty.

One talented young woman, Jasmine, age 14, said, "The hardest part about being a leader is the fear of failing or making a mistake… I hate the feeling of upsetting or letting someone down." Several heads around the room nodded in agreement. Even one of her leaders, Jessica, age 41, said, "What I find challenging about being a leader is the pressure of doing the job right… when you are a leader many people are depending on you."

CHILDHOOD FEMALE ARCHETYPES

CONSIDER THE FOLLOWING COMMON CHILDHOOD FEMALE ARCHETYPES:[17]

- The Pretty Princess – the performer who believes that appearance, helplessness, and coyness are her most powerful tools.
- The Wicked Witch – the "don't let anyone else get ahead of you" manipulator who moves ahead by pushing her peers down.
- Chicken Little – "the sky is falling" worrier who was so focused on what could go wrong that she cannot enjoy all that is going right.
- The Little Girl with the Curl – the "good girls are quiet and fit in" pleaser who has lost herself in trying to be what everyone else wants her to be.
- Little Red Hen – the "I'll do it myself" passive-aggressive martyr who has given up on asking for help or recognition and hides behind an unhealthy version of independence.
- Rapunzel – the victim who can't rescue herself, who is dependent on other, stronger, smarter, or braver types, and is caught in an unhealthy version of dependence.

As I read this list, I remember how often I had heard these stories growing up and how often I had told them to my children and others. No wonder our girls are confused.

REFLECTION – Were any of these messages part of your upbringing? If not, what messages were? Do you recognize any of them at work in your life now? What alternative archetype might be more helpful to you at this point in your journey?

If you are reading this as part of a book club or small group discussion prompt you might find it helpful to discuss the following questions together. If you are reading this book for personal enrichment you might want to use the following questions as a journaling exercise or consider gathering a group of friends this week to have coffee and discuss.

Soon, everywhere I turned, I began to see the high cost of women's low confidence. The implications are glaring. The reasons are deep-seated, destructive, and often divisive.

Consider that according to the Canadian Women's Foundation[18] a 2015 UN Human Rights report raised concerns about "the persisting inequalities between women and men" in Canada. This included the "high level of the pay gap" and its disproportionate effect on low-income women, visible minority and Indigenous women. Of the thirty-four countries studied, Canada had the seventh highest gender wage gap in 2014. According to Statistics Canada full-time women workers earn on average $0.72 for every dollar earned by men.[19] These statistics are not just about income as important as that may be. They are also about perceived value.

As well as the high cost of low confidence to individuals and families, a more hidden but still pervasive issue is the cost to society. While the true costs "are not easily quantifiable… they are very real."[20] The implications to organizations are becoming increasingly well documented. Catalyst, an independent research organization, has published multiple studies showing that "Fortune 500 firms… ranking in the top 25% in number of women board members generally have higher returns on equity sales, and working capital"[21] with stronger than average performance with three or more female board members.[22] A 2012 study, undertaken by the Credit Suisse Research Institute, shows that businesses with women on their boards outperformed comparably sized companies with all-male boards by 26 percent.[23] We know that more limited opportunities, less conducive cultures and many other factors contribute to the paucity of women at decision-making tables. Low confidence is both a result of and a contributing factor in this complex and systemic challenge. However, the result is clear: less diverse companies are less healthy companies. Women leaders are a business imperative.

An organization's financial viability is not all that is at stake. Two of my favorite advocates for diversity, Sally Helgeson and Julie Johnson, reported on their own and other women's aborted attempts to raise concerns about the factors that led to the 2008 economic downturn. They noted that,

A HUMAN RIGHT
(CONT'D)

Women can't afford to buy
into the myth of our own
inadequacy anymore.

"companies chose to view the retention of senior women as a women's issue rather than a strategic or leadership concern."[24] "[T]hey told us to wait… [that] we didn't know enough, didn't have the right credentials… weren't ready to serve on important boards… but some of the most qualified men in the world got us into this world-historic mess. Women can't afford to buy into the myth of our own inadequacy anymore!"[25] There is a reason why increasing numbers of people are acknowledging that "women constitute a business imperative."[26] Some people listened. Jacki Zechner, a former partner at Goldman Sachs, responded by funding a study observing that, "the companies needed more women leaders because they need a more balanced decision-making model."[27]

There is such a high cost to women's low confidence.

Helgeson commented that the inability of women to be able to fully engage in these companies should have been a warning sign long before any financial crisis occurred. The deterioration of values, company culture, and quality of life simultaneously drove women away and signaled impending problems for the organization.[28] Bridge Building Leaders cannot let this happen again.

The problem transcends business. Medical literature reveals a paucity of women as top faculty; the National Science Foundation reports there are few women in prestigious scientific positions; Bar associations cite low numbers of female partners in big law firms; Commissions at universities like John Hopkins, MIT, and Harvard find a lack of women among tenured faculty or at top academic ranks. Yet, each university or profession seems to think it has a unique problem.[29] Think about that for a moment. All these reports mention the same ingredients: the presence of few, if any, women role models in visible top positions; a lack of respect for women in general, including the different approaches they bring to the table; and inadequate or nonexistent policies on balancing family and work.[30] The challenge is not unique to any one culture or sector.

DISCUSS – what are the implications of the diverse, or non-diverse, decision making bodies in your line of work?

Discovering how to create environments in which both men and women leaders can thrive goes beyond diversity quotas and talent searches (as important as both of these may be) to fundamentally impact the fiber and potential of organizations.

DISCUSS – Why do you think teams of men and women are healthier and stronger? What strengths do women bring to business?

SOCIAL IMPLICATIONS

LOW SELF-ESTEEM HAS WIDESPREAD SOCIAL IMPLICATIONS. On a personal level it has been linked to violent behaviour, school dropout rates, teenage pregnancy, suicide, and low academic achievement.[31]

In our work at the Leadership Studio we see this first hand. One day a young woman we will call Anna participated in a leadership program. She sat in the back row, rarely raising her eyes, let alone her voice. Becoming increasingly concerned that we were not reaching this young woman, we sought to balance inviting her participation with respecting the discomfort she obviously felt when called on in any way. After three rounds of a 3-day program I worried we were exacerbating rather than relieving her angst. In the debriefing circle at the end of the final retreat I was wracking my brain to try to figure out how to allow her to contribute without embarrassing her. To our great surprise she volunteered a response. Her words were penetratingly profound.

She said, "I still don't think of myself as a leader. But I have begun to realize that, if I did, I would look at the whole world differently and that would change everything for me and maybe for others around me as well."

Twenty-four, normally rambunctious, high school aged students sat in the silence of that moment, looking at her with both compassion and respect. It was as if she had spoken on behalf of thousands of girls and women around the world.

Many sources insist that empowering women translates into community transformation. As early as the early 1990s the United Nations and World Bank began to appreciate the potential resource that women and girls represent. UNICEF issued a major report arguing that gender equality yields a "double dividend" by elevating not only women but also their children and communities. The Hunger Project proclaims, "Women are key to ending hunger in Africa." Doctors Without Borders asserts, "Progress is achieved through women."[32]

Meanwhile microenterprise non-profits discovered that when loans are made to women, they are not only much more likely to be repaid but also to cause systemic improvements in the whole community as women, now empowered by a cottage industry, begin to address the social needs of their community and their families.[33] Schools, clean water, health care facilities and other positive changes are much more likely to emerge and issues like crime and corruption decrease. The implications are staggering. A 1995 study[34] found that the status of women is a better predictor of quality of life for all than GDP, the conventional measure of a nation's economic development and overall health.[35] Think about that for a moment.

DISCUSS – What social justice issues might be resolved more quickly if both men and women were invited to decision making tables around the world?

WHERE WOMEN AND MEN ARE SERVING TOGETHER there are encouraging signs of community change.

MEN AND WOMEN TOGETHER CREATE COMMUNITY CHANGE

In India, having women in at least 30 percent of local policy making seats has had positive results in bringing about an "alternative vision of community development with the introduction of streetlights, clinics, libraries, and public toilets."[36] Due to the success at a local level, negotiations soon began to extend the concept to state and national levels.[37]

One study in the United States found that women in government are more likely, regardless of party, to concentrate on improving health care and education, ending violence, developing long-neglected supports for working families, fighting for better policies for women and bringing a different temperament to public policy discussions, with more listening and collaboration.[38]

A Critical Mass

"Money is a verb… it does things. It is not just something to have; it must build houses, schools, hospitals… and it must feed the people."

Luisa Diogo,
former Prime Minister
of Mozambique, and advocate
for infant health, gender
equality and free national
sexual health services.

IN 2015 I HAD THE PRIVILEGE OF ATTENDING some NGO meetings as part of the UN Commission on the Status of Women meetings in Manhattan. It was a strategic event. Fifteen years before, leaders from all over the world had set Millennial Goals and 189 countries around the world adopted them in an attempt to address the issues mentioned above. People gathered from the four-corners of the world. Walking the streets, one was apt to hear numerous languages spoken. New York maintains a high level of police presence, but with so many dignitaries in town there were even more.

A newbie, I sat in stunned silence as delegate after delegate waited patiently in line then respectfully and succinctly presented on the appalling situations their women and girls faced at home. Report after report noted how far their country had to go to reach the goals they had so ambitiously yet hopefully set fifteen years before. The tone of the room was somber. One director of a well-known NGO stood, not to report but to ask a question. With obvious disappointment in her voice she asked the panel what the NGO's could do better to help speed the progress. A government official stood to his feet and with obvious emotion thanked her for her question and her work. Scanning the thousands of delegates in the room, he said, "NGO's do not stop doing what you are doing. You are the ones holding our feet to the fire. Do not become discouraged. Without you, governments, who have so many priorities, restrictions, and powerful lobbying groups to please, would forget the importance of these issues and regress even further." He spoke as one more voice in a long line of voices that understood the importance and the challenges of this issue.

More than 30 years ago, Harvard Professor Rosabeth Moss Kanter first identified the importance of having a critical mass of at least one-third women in decision making roles to positively affect outcomes.[39] This advice was largely overlooked until 1995. Then in Beijing, at the fourth UN Conference on the Status of Women, a half-million delegates from 189 countries discussed the value of women's advancement in achieving major societal goals. Building on three years of regional research and expert input, they agreed that the presence of 30% women in decision-making bodies is the tipping point to have women's ideas, values, and approaches resonate. "The idea caught fire. A global agreement reaching across all cultures, religions, and political systems declared the importance of having 30% women decision makers to spur economic and social development."[40] Rarely has there been such widespread support behind a unifying approach.

Rosabeth Moss Kanter proposed that having fewer than 30% women in leadership creates an environment where those present tend to "act like male leaders" and are therefore not a good read of what female leaders actually look like.[41] She also suggested that teams with less than 30% women are less able to enact the changes a more balanced team would be able to achieve.[42]

Yet there we were, fifteen years later on the eve of a more diverse and healthy society; the much-anticipated Millennial Goals were reviewed and very few of those related to gender equality had been reached. Many in the room were angry, some disillusioned, some still idealistically hopeful. All agreed this is not a woman's issue. It is a humanity issue with widespread implications.

For conversely, and alarmingly, when women's voices are dismissed there are correlated social justice atrocities—especially to women and girls. The global statistics on the abuse of girls are numbing. Sex trafficking, forced prostitution, so-called honor killings, maternal mortality rates, female genital mutilation, aborted baby girls, and gender exclusive education are only some of the ramifications. It is not only women's issues that are affected, however. Some security experts note that countries that nurture terrorism "are disproportionately those where women are marginalized."[43]

A CRITICAL MASS
(CONT'D)

Meanwhile, including women in peacekeeping negotiations has been demonstrated to reduce conflict. Having women in local and national decision-making roles has been shown to increase organizational and national financial stability, create healthier and more humane cultures, and reduce crime and corruption.

Some sources suggest that many women are more comfortable in the centre of groups rather than at the top,[44] bonded by points of connection rather than "pecking orders."[45] This natural ability is invaluable to building healthy initiatives, organizations, and nations.

The shift in the past twenty years towards leadership that is visionary, participative, and coaching-oriented rather than control-based is sometimes referred to as Transformational leadership (vs. Transactional leadership).[46] A meta-analysis of forty-five studies suggests that women are more likely to be Transformational leaders than men.[47] Clearly gender diversity in corporate and community transformation is worth fighting for.

It is time to leverage the power of girls and women around the world.

DISCUSS – How do you respond to these stories and statistics?

REFLECT on Merida's quote – Do you agree? Disagree? If you were BRAVE enough to see it, what fate lives within you?

"There are those who say fate is something beyond our command, that destiny is not our own. But I know better. Our fate lives within us. You only have to be BRAVE enough to see it."

- Merida, in the movie *Brave*[48]

Since 2000 I have had the privilege of carrying out small, informal qualitative research groups in many parts of the world. One trip stands out. 30 days. 15 flights. 8 countries. Multiple languages. Numerous currencies. Innumerable and priceless interactions and insights.

Along the way we drank multiple cups of hot, sweet tea; visited carpet shops and a palace in Istanbul; read about the transformation of Warsaw in an airport hotel in Poland; shared a communal meal that transcended language barriers in Lithuania; spent an afternoon in the cathedral in Cologne; lost some luggage in Moscow; purchased handmade chocolate at an ancient monastery on a tiny island in the UK; and shared a Georgian Banquet under the stars, overlooking the Black Sea.

These small focus group discussions often became sacred places. Sometimes, it felt as if things were being said that up until now had not had a safe enough place to be spoken. When questions were asked about women in leadership, men and women, rather than answering directly, often shared stories. These were stories of their own pain, rejection and disillusionment but also stories of women who were having or have had great impact. In the Republic of Georgia I frequently heard stories of Queen Tamara, who reigned during the Golden Age of Georgia.[49] Ironically—being the first woman to reign on her own merits, and in spite of tremendous initial opposition—she was given the title "King" because no higher title could be thought of for her. When one participant shared this story no one commented on or seemed to even notice this irony.

It was not just the stories themselves but also the way they were told. They were told with pride, with admiration, with secret delight. As if men and women alike longed to see untold numbers of unlikely heroes find their voice and make a difference.

Some months after this trip, an invitation arrived to speak at another conference in Russia. It came from a woman who had not heard my workshops or been in one of the focus groups. In fact, the invitation had nothing to do with my teaching. It was extended because, when the workshop and focus group participants described the sessions to her they "sat up taller."

SACRED STORIES

Sharing their stories, they   had been reminded of the kind of leaders, and women, they were. These intimate dialogues provided a forum for me to examine the correlation between women's leadership roles, leadership confidence, and cultural norms—as demonstrated by their countries' rating on the World Economic Forum's longitudinal Gender Gap Index[50] study. This decades long study compares men's and women's realties in 130 countries. From bright and well-educated young women, to seasoned leaders, in Canada, Russia, Europe and Eastern Europe, now over a 15-year period, women I spoke to named "lack of confidence" as one of, if not the greatest obstacle to them stepping fully into their leadership capacity.

The suggestion that women leaders are more likely to lack confidence than their male peers is controversial. Yet both anecdotal stories and robust studies support my belief that this discrepancy exits.[51]

In fact, counter-intuitively to what we might anticipate, the more highly competent girls and women are, the more likely they are to underestimate their abilities.[52] This has important implications. For example, when confronted on why there were not more women in top civil service UN roles Former Secretary-General of the United Nations, Kofi Annan once said, "I've always been interested in seeing talented colleagues move up, and in my experience, many of them are women. So whenever an opening for a promotion was advertised, I often said to a talented person, 'You should apply for this job.' Women almost universally told me they weren't experienced enough or didn't have sufficient background. I never had a man say anything but 'Thank you, I will apply.'"[53]

In a 2015 study of 3,000 US, female college students and professional participants were asked about messages they had learned as a child. 86% recalled being told to be nice, to be respectful to others and to be a good student. 68% remember being coached to believe in themselves.

56% to take a stand for what they believed in.
44% to be a good leader.
39% to master a skill.[54]

When asked what contributed to their feelings of low confidence, women described the lack of congruity between stated and actual opportunities for them, the discrepancy between expectations of male and female leaders, the stereotypes and barriers they had faced and their internal angst about leadership as it was presented to them. Even more insidious are the mixed messages girls and women receive from birth.

One woman mused, "I wish I had learned that is okay to be nice to people and be a leader."

PERSONAL REFLECTION – What messages did you receive as a child around leadership, speaking up and courage?

Magnify these messages on a global level and consider the realities many women face. Gender related issues begin pre-birth and continue throughout the decades of a woman's life. These issues impact women to varying degrees based on their geographical, cultural, monetary, and family context. Globally, however, they add up; such that women become increasingly aware that to be female is often to be considered lesser… other.

The messages are both subtle and glaring. More girls are killed in routine "gendercide"—babies aborted because of their gender, honor killings, complications from female genital mutilation etc.—in any one decade than people have been slaughtered in all genocides of the 20th C.[55] In many parts of the world, female babies are seen as a greater financial burden than boys, although, equally horrific, this is changing in places where human trafficking of young virgins makes having girls financially desirable for families. Throughout their lives women are significantly more likely to be impacted by poverty, domestic violence, sexual abuse, and human trafficking.[56]

The issue of human trafficking has rocked many of our worlds. It is almost unbelievable that this issue could be growing so exponentially that the number of human slaves today far exceeds that of the Transatlantic trade. I remember sitting in history class in school thinking, "If this were happening in my day I would have done something about it." And yet here I was, age 50, just learning the extent of the systemic problem that is literally and metaphorically raping our generation.

A friend from Eastern Europe sat at our dining room table sipping tea. He told us about the rescue and prevention work he and his wife, and their team of seventy staff, led in Moldova. The statistics were staggering. Yet, as is often the case, it was not until he told a story that the fire in my belly flared up enough to cause me to act. He shared that at that time it was not uncommon for people to visit seriously under-resourced orphanages to choose young girls who stood out for their beauty, innocence, and intelligence. Underpaid and desperate directors were paid extra to take special care of these children so that a few years later, better fed and educated they would earn more money when sold.

> The poorest country in Europe.
> Organized crime supported by bribes at high levels.
> Vulnerable children in a vulnerable system.
> Personal greed.
> A recipe for atrocity.

Discuss – What global atrocities make your skin crawl? What connection can you see between our silence and others' suffering? How might our purchasing or other aspects of our lifestyle actually be contributing to the problem?

Building Brave Leadership

A 2008 GIRL SCOUTS OF THE USA study found that girls believe a leader is defined not only by the qualities and skills they have, but also by how those qualities and skills are used to make a difference. Those who think like Bridge Building Leaders agree. In the girls' own words, they want to be the type of leader who "stands up for his or her beliefs and values," and "tries to change the world for the better." In this model, leadership is "knowing what you believe and putting it into action."[57] They also found that girls are more likely than boys to want to be leaders in order to help other people (67% vs. 53% for boys), share their knowledge and skills with others (53% vs. 45%), and change the world for the better (45% vs. 31%).[58]

DISCUSS – How does what you believe inform your leadership? How is your leadership changing the world for the better?

POSITIVE CHANGE

POWERFUL CONTEXT

IN THE LEADERSHIP STUDIO, we observe huge breakthroughs in thinking and behaviour when girls and women are given the opportunity to discuss their leadership journey with different generations. Something magical happens when women reflect on what has crafted their identity as leaders. Expand this onto the millions of women who live around the world—many in situations much more dire than our own—and a sense of the scale of the challenge and the potential emerges.

Another powerful breakthrough happens when women perceive how their fears influence girls coming after them. Many women, unwilling to speak up for themselves, will speak up for the girls they care about. One of the most important things you, as a Bridge Building Leader, can do for yourself and our world is to consider mentoring your daughter, niece, or young friend on her leadership journey. As we have said, a young woman's sense of self starts early. The development of a leadership mindset has important, specific aspects at grade three, six through eight, and then again throughout high school. A girl's definition of leadership, and her ability to lead, changes with age. Elementary school aged girl's view leadership as, "what I can do." In middle school this changes to, "how I can impact others." Then in high school leadership becomes more, "inner-directed again with an emphasis on confidence... [and] who I am as a leader."[59] This knowledge is a great foundation for helping a young woman's leadership development.

Elementary school aged girls need to be exposed to lots of different types of opportunities and learn the important skill of failing forward.[60] Otherwise, fear of failure becomes a strong deterrent to their willingness to influence the world around them.

In middle school, girls need opportunities to build and participate on teams. Many girls—and women—prefer to be part of an all-star team than to be the all-star of a team. This has important implications for how we coach athletics, arts, academics—especially STEM (Science, Technology, Engineering and Math) based activities and community service or social justice initiatives. Helping girls create projects that enable collaboration to make a difference ingrains the powerful and motivating principle that, "together we can make a difference." This corresponds to the changes that occur for girls around grade six, when they begin intentionally changing themselves in order to fit in. Why not change the environment so they don't have to?

In grades nine through twelve, girls engage in an inner journey that takes them deep into issues of identity, preference, worth, and belonging. Like girls in younger grades, they need mature women in their lives who can help navigate such challenging terrain. Self-awareness and self-regulation should be balanced by external goals that help protect young women from becoming too internally focused, self-conscious, or perfectionist in their approach.

WE SHOULD NOT MINIMIZE THE POWER OF PEERS or the number of mean girls in many high school settings. Many bright, athletic, and beautiful young women become scarred by the messages they hear just because they are good at something. We sometimes call this the Tall Poppy Syndrome. Inherent in many cultures, there is a fundamental fear of standing out. This is based on the human tendency to sabotage any "tall poppies" that dare to poke their heads above the rest of the field. At the very least, we tend to leave them unprotected up there above us, to increase the likelihood that they will fall. This can take the form of snickers and arched eyebrows, expulsion from cliques, de-friending, and the retraction of social invitations. These are both incredibly common and destructive for many competent and even previously well-liked girls.

TALL POPPY SYNDROME

Tall Poppy Syndrome.
Smart Girl Syndrome.
Bullying by Mean Girls intent on preserving the status quo and themselves as the queen of it.
Imposter Syndrome.
Double binds.
Impossible standards of body image.

It is a wonder and a testimony to their resilience that our girls survive at all.

It takes a village to raise a leader, especially a BRAVE Bridge Building Leader. And statistically, the villages our girls are growing up in are subtly or even overtly antagonistic to their development. Don't stand back and watch. Step in. Tell your story. Offer support. Provide alternative environments and activities. Help bring perspective. Coach a team. Start a club. Take a young girl out for lunch. These years are critical and girls need positive adult involvement if they are going to thrive. Certainly this is the window for some of their most significant leadership development. One study found that pre-college leadership experiences—training, involvement in high school student groups, volunteer service, varsity sports, and positional leadership roles and values—were found to yield the highest correlation to college and post-college leadership outcomes.[61]

ASK A GIRL

ASK A GIRL – Set up a teatime with your daughter, granddaughter, or a group of young friends to talk about leadership. Ask what they think makes a good leader and how they see themselves as leaders. Stay in a position of listening. Seek to truly understand their dreams and fears. Authentically enourage them. Record any insights here.

LEFT ALONE, GIRLS' LEADERSHIP CONFIDENCE WILL DECREASE as they grow up. This is a huge problem, causing them to "under-invest, to under-inno-vate, and to assume that everything is stacked against them, so there is no point in trying."[62] Sadly, the trend continues into adulthood.

While sixty-nine percent of young girls (the same percentage as boys) con-sider themselves leaders, only thirty-six percent are interested in being a leader when they get older.[63] There is also a strong correlation between the beliefs we have in our own ability and how well we will perform a task or range of actions.[64] Betz and Hackett have explored this phenomenon as it relates to women's career development.[65] Their work shows a close link between a woman's perceived self-efficacy and her career decisions and success. People with higher levels of confidence are more apt to take risks and persevere through the inevitable obstacles that one encounters in life and leadership.

Ironically, I was terrified to speak to a gathering of female STEM lead-ers about Stages of Personal Power and leadership confidence. The idea of standing in front of a room full of Ph.D.'s—in a field I knew little about—whose experiences had been so different from mine, felt completely over-whelming. With "kick in the butt" type encouragement from friends, I made it there. However, with the massive lectern looming between me and the audience, half the group trickling in late from coffee break, and coming after a powerhouse complement of competent speakers, my Lizard Brain overpowered my rational one. I could barely read, let alone remember my carefully rehearsed talk. In a foolish attempt to impress I was using a tech-nology I was less familiar with. The new clothes I was wearing felt uncom-fortable. Only my daughter's reminder as I stepped on the plane—that even if I bombed I would probably never see these women again—gave me courage to step onto the platform. Every eye turned towards me. The room grew quiet. I felt my voice tighten but forced myself to breathe, and then to smile, and then to speak. Somehow I got through it. Knowing I had not hit it out of any park, I slunk back to my seat. Head down, I listened to the final announcements and plotted how best to get back to my room without having to pass anyone. Then I looked up. A long line of women stood waiting to talk.

PERCEPTIONS AND ABILITIES

Throughout the next twenty-four hours, and even as I walked towards my taxi to the airport, women sidled up to me with words like, "I have never told anyone this before," or, "you named what I have been sensing for years," or, "I don't want my daughters to experience what I have, what would you suggest?" These were scientists from NASA, Deans of Universities, researchers and authors, heads of NGOs, and executives from huge for-profit organizations. Even though I had been researching this issue for years, I was still stunned. Apparently I was not the only one lacking confidence in the room that day.

How Confidence Grows

THE QUESTION OF HOW CONFIDENCE GROWS is complex. Freelance writer Olivia Barrow writes of her High School Literature teacher's formula for why some people are happy and others are not: Expectations – Reality = Insecurity. Expectations are certainly a key factor, as are perceptions. As the research on girl's confidence quoted earlier suggests, upbringing and culture are key factors that contribute to this. Psychologist Albert Bandura also offers four sources of self-efficacy, offered here in decreasing level of impact:

1. MASTERY EXPERIENCES—which, as the words suggest, involves personal success. This requires opportunities to test skill sets, something many women express they are not being given.

2. VICARIOUS EXPERIENCES—seeing people who are similar to us succeed at things we would like to do. This is influenced by the similarity of the other person—gender and ethnicity being significant factors. Women in many fields note the scarcity of strong women leader role models. Yet according to Bandura's theory, "people seek proficient models who possess the competencies to which they aspire."[66] I would add that many women also seek models that carry out the competencies in ways that align to their values. We know that "most human behavior is learned through modeling: from observing others, one forms an idea of how new behaviors are performed, and on later occasions this coded information serves as a guide for action."[67] We also know that one's environment impacts one's behaviour and one's behaviour impacts one's environment.[68] This is keenly seen in the situation of women leaders.

3. SOCIAL PERSUASION—encouragement from others, whose opinion we respect, that says we are capable. Given that many women grow through affirmation, there is a definite need to accentuate positive reinforcement in their leadership journey. Yet, many women speak of the mixed messages, lack of support, and minimal encouragement they receive as a woman leader. This is accentuated by the fact that "it is more difficult to instill high levels of personal efficacy by social persuasion than to undermine it."[69]

4. EMOTIONAL STATUS—our ability to stay positive and manage stress in healthy ways, such that we are more likely to have the personal margin to try new things, take risks and recover or learn from failure. Many women speak of being dismissed for expressing emotion and being asked to work in ways that undermine their values. This impacts their ability to stay emotionally healthy and authentic. They also noted the challenges of developing a network and finding mentors, making them feel alone.

These four sources illustrate both the problem and the potential. Consider, for example, the influence on expectations and follow-through. According to Bandura, "The higher the perceived self-efficacy, the higher the goal-challenges people set for themselves and the firmer their commitment to them."[70] Yet, even this does not tell the whole story. For women, a lifetime of mixed messages, a growing awareness of the global mistreatment of women purely because of their gender, and many other factors, make this a vastly complex and deep issue.

No wonder many women are struggling. No wonder our organizations and communities are paying the price. No wonder (I tell my bank account) I went back to school at the age of fifty to wrestle more deeply with the problem and the potential.

Hundreds of hours and thousands of dollars later, I would like to offer a model of what I believe outlines the key factors and forces that encourage women to become BRAVE Bridge Building Leaders.

THE NON-LINEAR PATH OF WOMEN LEADERS

LIKE ANY MODEL IT IS VASTLY OVERSIMPLIFIED. It may not reflect your reality. The model seeks to represent both internal and external factors, as the one naturally informs the other. It stresses the importance of a culture-shifting paradigm, since the complexity and longevity of the issue requires a systemic approach. I respectfully submit it for your consideration as an invitation to continue the discussion. I have drawn the model as a square, representing a decision-making table that shrinks or expands according to seven factors.

Inside the square are the two factors that most influence many women's level of motivation and sense of satisfaction: purposeful work and a collegial setting. Bridge Building Leaders are more willing to lead in settings where they perceive the work to be meaningful than in settings where status or symbols are used as motivators.

Women are also more willing to lead when the environment is collegial. By this we mean many women prefer relationship rich settings where they can work as part of high-performing team that has at least thirty-percent women, where diversity is celebrated and there are multiple female role models and mentors. Women speak frequently about the importance of being included in formal meetings, opportunities, and processes as well as in the informal activities where relationship building and decision-making often occur.

Leading into the square, a wavey line represents the nonlinear path many women have followed to the place of their current influence. This path begins early, as we have seen, and is informed not ony by their personal journey but also by those around them—their parents, their heritage, their peers, and to a certain extent, the story of women over time and across boundaries. The path will be shorter for some than others but it is not uncommon for women's leadership to peak in their forties and fifties, long after their male peers. It is generally believed that women take ten years longer than men, on average, to recognize how competent they are at leading.

Bounding the square are four important interrelated, internal—but externally influenced—factors: affirmation of strengths and value, invitation to contribute, opportunity to discover one's voice, and opportunity to develop self-efficacy.

It is therefore drawn like this.

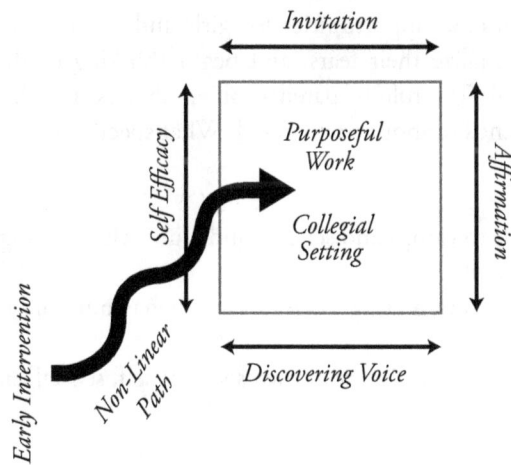

Figure 1. Women leaders' confidence enhancing model.

Related to the importance of a collegial culture is the important finding that women are more likely to grow through affirmation than through challenge. For women, affirmation comes first, challenge after. As Adrienne Rich writes, "Every woman, regardless of age, social class, ethnicity, and academic achievement, needs to know that she is capable of intelligent thought… Many of the women we interviewed had not yet learned [this]. In the masculine [model] confirmation comes… at the end…

For women confirmation and community are prerequisites rather than consequences of development." [71]

WE KNOW THAT "THE EARLY YEARS OF A WOMAN'S LIFE, their experience of being female, and the significance of female influences in shaping their future figure particularly prominently in women leaders' experiences."[72] And we know that "The messages women imbibe, which may lead them to doubt their calling as leaders, start young. Early adolescence is the time when many girls begin to silence themselves, letting others speak for them and allowing other voices to usurp the value of their own voice."[73]

Frequent and intentional opportunities for girls and women to discover their strengths, normalize their fears, and begin thinking of themselves as leaders are critical. The role of parents, older siblings, female cousins, role models and friends cannot be overstated. What specific behaviours are most helpful?

> Exposing girls to camps and schools and clubs where young women lead well.
> Calling out and celebrating the leadership behaviours and mindsets you see in them.
> Developing and modeling your own sense of self, self-efficacy and self-leadership.

It takes a great deal of intentionality to balance the messages that initiative in girls is actually bossy-ness, that girls must choose between being liked and being respected,[74] and that girls who speak up are left out.

Considering the mixed messages many girls and women receive, and the scarcity of female leadership role models, many women bring unhealthy baggage with them into the leadership forum. Once at the table, many find even less support, more scrutiny, and ongoing conflicting messages. No wonder many women feel the deck is stacked against them.

GIRLS THINK DIFFERENTLY ABOUT LEADERSHIP THAN THEIR MALE PEERS. Programs designed for the way they think and learn are therefore crucial. Those wishing to reverse current trends must do so intentionally; however, this is not always easy. A young woman came four times to one of our early programs. Each time she had demonstrated solid leadership behaviours: leading her peers in activities, speaking up for what she believed was right, and helping those new to the program to fit in and benefit most from it. Proud of her, and of the progress we had seen in her, we began to speak into her during the final debrief. To our surprise she completely shut down under our affirmation. She denied that she was a leader or had influenced her peers. She was embarrassed at being singled out and uncomfortable with the pressure she perceived was being put on her.

APPROPRIATE, EARLY
INTERVENTION

We have often observed this response in promising young women. What is going on here? The reactions are no doubt as complex and varied as the young women themselves but three factors have often been observed:

1. Many girls over the age of 9 or 10 years dislike and fear being singled out in front of their peers—even for positive behaviours. Sadly, the additional pressure of perceived increased expectations sometimes undermines the encouragement. Ingrained responses to the Mean Girl, Tall Poppy, Bossy Girls or Smart Girl Syndromes described earlier can be complicating factors. While culture,[75] personality type,[76] and love languages[77] obviously influence the degree to which this is true for individuals, many girls prefer being acknowledged privately for individual success and publically only when the contribution of the whole group is being celebrated. For young women feeling this way we find that quietly affirming and demonstrating that you are on her side enables them to more likely appreciate and accurately interpret a nod of approval and smile of encouragement next time.

2. Many girls are not very self-aware—or at least not when it comes to their strengths. They are much more aware of and comfortable talking about their weaknesses and flaws. There is perhaps no more powerful gift to give young leaders than genuine feedback about their strengths.

In the Studio, we do a simple exercise that enables girls to tell their story in a visual format. At the end of the exercise they are encouraged to share whichever pieces they feel comfortable sharing. In our experience very few will share strengths and successes. Yet when we ask these same girls to pass their closed work around so that others can record the strengths they see in them on the outside of their piece, the room turns silent and additional time is requested. The looks on girls faces as they read the strengths their peers see in them is truly astounding. Without fail many girls will describe the insights they gain from this part of the exercise, and breakthrough these insights provided, as the highlight of their time with us. The power of positive peer affirmation cannot be underestimated when it comes to helping girls see their strengths.

3. Many girls fear the responsibility and loneliness of leadership. Understanding the implications of leading others astray, and believing they must choose between influencing others and being liked by others, many girls—even those practicing leadership behaviours—will deny their leadership ability and actions. Here again we find that envisioning leadership as behaviour, rather than an elevated position, and celebrating what we can do together is a far more effective strategy for many girls' leadership development.

4. Many girls (and adults) are looking for affirmation from the very people least likely to give it—the mean girls, the boys club, or the impossible-to-please coach, teacher or parent. We tend to dismiss the words of those who we think, "have to say that" and listen to those who are either putting others down to mask their insecurity or are unaware of the impact of their words. We find that coaching the "people who count to that girl" about both why and how to speak into her can be a very powerful strategy, assuming they are willing. Intergenerational events can be powerful opportunities to accomplish this.

5. Faith and family may also be factors. One US study revealed that adolescents who regularly attended religious institutions are more likely to have higher self-esteem than their peers.[78] The same study stressed the role of family as significant in nurturing one's view of self.

WHEN IT COMES TO ENCOURAGING THE LEADERSHIP DEVELOPMENT of women early intervention is critical and so is a long-term approach. For any number of personal and cultural reasons many women don't truly peak as leaders until their forties or older. For many women, it is not until after family responsibilities are less all encompassing and age and experience have allowed for fresh perspective that they move into places of empowered and empowering leadership.

Unfortunately, many models of career development[79] are linear; demonstrating traditional male values of career centricity; and separating work and family life. For a variety of life and worldview reasons, women tend not to adopt this framework.

> Women are more likely to consider how career choices will impact their family.[80]
> Women's lives are marked by distinct seasons;[81] each is filled with competing and variable priorities.

These factors contribute to many women's need to frequently reinvent themselves. While that is a powerful and important opportunity it may also, in some cases, lead to low levels of confidence, for example when re-entering the work force.

Sadly, we minimize the skills, perspectives and character development that often accompanies long-term care of children, the elderly, or the sick. This is craziness. If I were to start a new company today, I would hire only people who had spent an extended period of time in one of these settings. There are important things that can best be learned in these unique contexts and anyone who has done well there would be at the front of my hiring line.

We are beginning to see how the correlation between the importance of early intervention in girls lives, the diverse seasons of many women's lives, and the non-linear path of many women's leadership suggests that tremendous intentionality must be put into developing girls' and young women who may not peak as leaders for another twenty or thirty years. Such intentionality is rare. Sadly, this contributes to the long and often painful self-awareness journey towards the external opportunity, and internal courage, to lead.

THE IMPORTANCE OF PURPOSEFUL WORK

MARCUS BUCKINGHAM SURVEYED 1.3 MILLION PEOPLE about their quality of life. His findings dispel the common belief that women, as a result of better education, jobs, and pay are happier and more fulfilled than they were forty years ago. Instead, he found that women are less happy, more rushed, and more stressed than our mothers were and more stressed than their male peers.[82] As if this was not bad enough a follow up study demonstrated that women become less satisfied with every aspect of their lives as they get older.[83] These findings are disturbing but perhaps not surprising. Many women feel like they are drowning.

Drowning in the expectations they set for themselves.
Drowning in the expectations others seem to have set for them.
Drowning in details and deadlines.
Drowning in complicated relationships and controversial decision-making.
Drowning in corporate and community cultures not designed by or for them.

PERSONAL REFLECTION – Are there any areas of your life where you feel like you are drowning? What has been your approach to stay above water? How well is that working for you?

In the Buckingham study the factor that made the biggest difference was the commitment level of women to be true to themselves, to discover what strengthens them, and to allow this to guide their choices and life journey[84] rather than living a second rate version of someone else's life.[85] Wow, let that sink in for a moment. Authenticity and purposeful work could not be more closely linked!

PERSONAL REFLECTION – Where might I be living a second-rate version of someone else's life? What do I want to do about this?

PERSONAL REFLECTION – Where have I given myself the freedom to be completely authentic? Where have I not—and why? Where do I believe I am making a meaningful difference in the world? What is stopping me from leaning more fully into work that has deep meaning for me?

It is not that that purposeful work is not important to men as well—just the opposite—men and women equally share this need. Bridge Building Leaders understand this and leverage it to empower personal enrichment and global change. As Victor Frankl once said, *"Being human always points to something, or someone, other than oneself… what [humanity] actually needs is not a tensionless state but rather the striving and struggling for a worthwhile goal, a freely chosen task."*

PERSONAL REFLECTION – How does the work you are doing align to something bigger than yourself? Where have you helped others to align their contribution to a greater purpose?

This is not a new concept. Many ancient cultures understood the importance of seeking out that which is meaningful and dedicating our lives to it. One of my favorite expressions of this comes from New Zealand.

Whāia e koe ki iti kahurangi;
ki te tuohu koe me he maunga teitei.
Seek the treasure you value most dearly;
If you bow your head, let it be to a lofty mountain.
Māori Proverb

Numerous other studies demonstrate the importance of purposeful work.[86] Meaning transcends an inspirational vision statement and it is not only found in non-profits or service-oriented vocations. Meaning can be found in any sector and Bridge Building Leaders are skilled at unearthing and maximizing it's potential.

PERSONAL OR GROUP REFLECTION – If I were to choose three to five themes that reflect the kind of environment where I personally thrive, they would be:

THE ROLE OF RICH
RELATIONSHIPS

IF YOU HAVE LEFT A JOB BECAUSE OF THE LOW QUALITY OF RELATIONSHIPS, you are not alone. While relationship rich environments may seem equally important to men and women it turns out this is not quite true. In one study of twenty-one career values, regardless of age, "the most significant difference between genders was the importance of social interactions in the workplace."[87] A Roosevelt University study found that "a relationship-oriented climate" was the number one factor in determining a woman's commitment to an organization.[88] Other research found that women, unlike their male peers, reported valuing social interaction and the relationships they formed at work as more satisfying than monetary rewards.[89] Not surprisingly then, targeted studies of successful female entrepreneurs suggest they build "relationship-centric" organizations in order to build loyalty among female staff members.[90]

BRAVE leaders go beyond everyday friendship and partnership building. They build radical relationships. They are skilled at building the kind of bridges between diverse people and perspectives that can lead to transformation.

Friendships are important. For BRAVE Bridge Building Leaders they serve at least two very important roles.

1. Friendships challenge us: Female friendships can actually help women develop their intellectual capacities and become better scholars.[91] Friendships are particularly important for women of colour as a way to "build and protect self-esteem within a racist and an ethnocentric institutional culture."[92]
2. Friendships mirror for us: Friends help us see who we really are and to see others in new fresh ways. Feminist developmental frameworks present a view of women's self-authorship as a function of empathetic relationships and not through ideals of self-sufficiency and isolated reflection.[93]

Not only do friendships create a place for intellectual stimulation, wisdom, confidence building and self-authorship in college, they become increasingly important as women navigate the changes associated with moving into careers and significant relationships.[94]

The value of intimacy in female friendship demonstrates that environments are critical in meeting our developmental needs[95] and is supported by feminist scholarship on the psychological development of girls and women[96] across the life span.[97]

While critical for women this kind of culture is good for all of us. Gallup's Tom Rath, author of *StrengthsFinder 2.0* pored over 8-million interviews and numerous other research projects to discover that people with a best friend at work are seven times more likely to be engaged in their job and that people with 3-4 what he called "vital friends" at work produce more, are happier, and even healthier.[98]

I am one of those fortunate women who have amazing friends. I hope you are too. The word friend in Old English was related to two words: *freond*, which means "to love" and its root word *freo,* which means "free."

In Arabic, it was also related to two concepts: "the one who accompanies" and "the one who tells the truth."

Combining these two worldviews we create a fascinating definition of friendship:

> A friend is someone who loves you enough to walk beside you
> *and tell you the kind of truth that sets you free.*

Imagine the potential for relationships that provide this kind of insight.

THE ROLE OF RICH
RELATIONSHIPS
(CONT'D)

PERSONAL REFLECTION – Who are the friends that help you to see yourself as you truly are and challenge you to be your best self?

The isolation leaders feel is often exacerbated for woman. The importance of relationship rich environments has other implications for female leaders as well. Consider women's "tend and befriend (vs. men's more well known "fight or flight") response to stress."[99] Consider the high turnover of women leaders in almost every sector. While this has often been attributed to low pay or inflexible hours Joanna Barsch and Susie Cranston carried out a multi-year study—including hundreds of interviews and almost 2,000 male and female executives polled—and found that women with strong networks and mentors "enjoy more promotions, higher pay, and greater work satisfaction. In particular women leaders benefit from professional development and active career support."[100]

Of course not all cultures minimize the importance of relationships to leadership the way the West has. Many Indigenous communities share a deeply relational worldview—which stands in sharp contrast to the philosophy that undergirds Western individualistic economic and political thinking. In Māori this relational worldview is expressed as *whakapapa*. Navaho's describe it as *hozho*. While each of these words has different nuanced meaning they share the common core of the importance of connectedness.[101]

Adrienne Clarkson, Former Governor General of Canada, asks, "What is the paradox of citizenship? The paradox is that we are most authentically ourselves, most truly human, when we commit to and engage with the community."[102] She adds, "We have lived so long with the Cartesian idea ['I think therefore I am'] that it has all but blinded us to the concept of what it is to be a person in all human manifestations."[103]

DISCUSS – How has your view of independence and interdependence in leadership been influenced by the prevailing worldview of your culture?

THE CONCEPT OF UBUNTU IS AN ETHICAL VALUE that is difficult to express in English or to understand from a Western perspective. It originated with Bantu peoples and has been upheld by African societies for millennia. Unlike our individualistic Western approach, Ubuntu teaches, "I am what I am because of what others have been in the past, and what I am now in the present will be part of the future."[104] Or more simply, "I am because we are."[105] In the traditional context, leaders were more likely to succeed if they were deeply spiritual, accepted diversity, were close to their people and involved their people in decisions that affected them—allowing for significant discussion and debate.[106]

UBUNTU: I AM BECAUSE WE ARE

Perhaps Nelson Mandela is the best-known example of this mindset. Nelson was raised to be a chief of the Thembu nation. As a young man he used his skills as a lawyer to defy apartheid and, as a result, spent 27 years in prison, emerging to not only lead his nation into a new era but also to demonstrate a new style of leadership. He demonstrated a level of courageous Bridge Building Leadership rarely seen in the public forum. Being steeped in Ubuntu no doubt influenced much of his thinking, yet we can't help but reflect that so many others shared his heritage but were unable to make the leap he did. Nelson teaches us that only those who have gone deep, who have suffered—and not only endured but also been transformed—can truly become Bridge Building Leaders who can themselves lead transformational change.

In traditional African wisdom "leadership is about loving your people… [a leader's] major function is to ensure an environment that promotes trust and goodwill amongst their people… [and] groups that then form a greater family, community or nation… Successful leaders therefore had to develop the wisdom, art and skill to unite people. In good times and bad."[107]

There is so much about this worldview that is interesting to consider. It is best envisioned as a co-creation process of being human in a spirit of fellowship, humanity, and compassion.[108] In no way does this minimize the importance of self however. In fact, it starts with the realization that being human involves a high level of self-awareness, self-confidence (rooted in our heritage), and self-motivation, enabling us to more fully understand and recognize other human beings.[109] People who are practicing Ubuntu will not necessarily hold an official role but will have found a way to position themselves in any situation so they can play a positive role that enhances the good of the community. Ubuntu teaches that you cannot be fully human if you cannot practice self-control or are intolerant of other perspectives or speeds of action.[110] This kind of thinking is at the heart of BRAVE Bridge Building Leadership.

If you have ever balked at productivity audits, rushed meetings, decisions made with one bottom line in mind or mandatory time-management seminars you may be interested to know that Ubuntu leaders, like many Indigenous peoples across North America, understood their world in a significantly non-Western way. They believed that they owned time—rather than time owning them—and were therefore willing to take the time it took to build trust, seek counsel from all interested parties, and build consensus. "Deep dialogue was such an art form and key ingredient of legitimate leadership, that every Afrikan culture has a version of the dialogue process of *dare* (in Shona), *tinkhundla, indaba, imbizo* (in isiZulu) or *pitso*.[111] We will explore this further when we discuss Peter Senge's seminal work on learning communities. For now it is enough to note that Senge reaches back into these ancient traditions to explore the power of true dialogue, deep learning, and transformational breakthroughs.

REFLECTION – What questions, concerns and inspirations run through your head as you reflect on how contextualizing these concepts in your setting might unfold?

Bridge Building Leaders can also learn from both current and ancient worldviews that balance the strengths of men and women, old (experience and wisdom) and young (passion, energy and enthusiasm). In many cultures the young were expected to defer to the older generation in any areas where their elders have experienced or mastered something. Older generations were often to defer to younger in areas where they had no significant experience or where more active creativity or action was required.

Understanding these core-values enables us to understand how leadership would naturally unfold. For example, elders often initiated decision-making dialogue, while the youth observed. In some African communities older leaders provided as much wisdom as they could and provided the context and guidelines on how the community would normally behave in such situations. Then they would turn to the youth and say in effect, "You are the young blood. You think faster, act faster, and have clearer eyes than we do. Having heard all we have to say what do you think?" Normally this would end with the youth being given a full mandate from the elders to implement the solution.[112]

In a recent visit to New Zealand I discovered a similar rich history. In traditional Māori culture each community was ruled by a *rangatira* (Māori Aristocracy) led by the chief. The literal meaning of *rangatira* is "to weave people together"; a definition of leadership that encapsulates the interdependent and collectivist nature of Māori society.[113] There is much in these ancient ways of thinking to inform ours today. However, information alone is not enough. In a recent study of New Zealand leaders, Māori participants scored their leaders higher on three of the five dimensions of transformational leadership than non-Māori participants scored their non-Māori leaders.[114] Exposure and proximity were not enough to change behaviour and mindsets. The insight is obvious and painful, only those skilled in and intentional about Bridge Building will be able to internalize the principles most needed in our generation.

REFLECTION – What inspires you about the examples and stories given here? How might that be contextualized into your Bridge Building Leadership?

Of course, I am not suggesting that relationships are not important to Western men. Many male teams rise and fall on this principle. Legendary Coach of the NFL football team the Greenbay Packers, Vince Lombardi, once said, "The challenge of every team is to build a feeling of oneness, of dependence on one another, because the question is usually not how well each person performs but how well they perform together."[115]

However, when it comes to creating environments where women thrive, this factor becomes incredibly important to those who understand the potential of balanced leadership practices. This is strengthened by the many studies that link interconnectedness to transformational leadership and transformational leadership to increased job satisfaction and longevity,[116] as well as organizational change.[117]

The Tall Poppy Grows up

BEFORE LEAVING THIS TOPIC, it is crucial for us to revisit the lesson of the Tall Poppy. This phenomenon does not disappear after high school. Why is this? No doubt the reasons are deep seated and primal, but one reason is clear. When we lack confidence ourselves we seek to pull down those around us. In so doing of course we only increase the level of mediocrity and rob ourselves, and our children, of the opportunity to see greatness. BRAVE women resist this childish desire. BRAVE women start building scaffolds of support when their peers begin to rise.

How do we create cultures that support women leaders? The English word culture comes from the German *Kultur*, meaning to develop or grow. It was used in Greek philosophy, but was not used anthropologically until the nineteenth-century.[118] Using culture as a way of thinking about work environments is even more recent. It has become important in leadership thinking. Yet what do we mean when we talk about national or organizational culture?

Culture is like the water that fish swim in. It can be healthy or un-healthy, hot or cold, salt or fresh, and yet for the fish that have become used to it is almost unobservable. This dynamic, deeply influential, multifaceted and often unstated concept is both pervasive and powerful. Leaders often unintentionally create cultures that work for some but not for all. Bridge Building Leaders understand the importance of an intentionally inclusive cultural design.

Discuss – In what ways does knowing the root meaning of the word culture (to develop or grow) cause you to think differently about it? If we were to think of it as essentially a conversation among diverse people how would this cause you to think about both culture and culture change?

ORGANIZATIONAL
CULTURE

ORGANIZATIONAL
CULTURE
(CONT'D)

The culture of an organization, community, or nation radically impacts the confidence of its women. It influences expectations—a factor previously noted as critical to confidence building. In one study seventy-nine percent of all mid- or senior-level women agreed they wanted to reach top management—just two percentage points lower than their male peers. Senior women executives were more even likely to agree strongly. Yet only sixty-nine percent of these same senior leaders said they were confident they'd be successful, as opposed to eighty-six percent of their male peers.

The same study found that a favorable environment and cultural factors weighed twice as heavily as individual factors in determining how confident women felt about reaching top management.

Why would that be?

Women who are more confident of their ability to rise are more likely to say that the leadership styles of their companies are compatible with women's leadership and communication styles, and that women are just as likely as men to reach the top there. Yet almost forty percent of female respondents said that women's leadership and communication styles don't fit with the prevailing model of top management in their companies.[119] This insight is so important. It is not that only women who lack confidence are less likely to succeed. Women, intuitively reading the culture of their organization, lower the expectation of advancement to match the likelihood that their style of leadership is valued and will be supported at that level.

A related study found that men's perception of women leaders is still a significant hurdle. While three-quarters of men agreed that diverse leadership teams generate better company performance, 77% of female respondents strongly agreed that women can lead as effectively as men at C Levels but only 50% of men.[120] Many men chose agree over strongly agree and it is in the nuanced transition that we see the subtle, unspoken challenge. Men were also almost six times more likely than their female peers to disagree it is more difficult for women to make it as a leader.[121]

DISCUSS – How has your culture impacted your view of yourself as a leader?

REFLECT on how one's culture creates a lens through which we view and interact with the world.

DISCUSS – How does culture change? What are the culture drivers in your organization?

"When asked about the most important drivers for increasing gender diversity at the top, executives identify two in particular: strong CEO and top-management commitment, and a corporate culture that support gender-diversity objectives. The complexity of the issues ensures that there is no single way to make change happen; companies need a whole ecosystem of measures. However, change starts at the top—and respondents recognize how important this leadership support is."[122]

"Culture does not change because we desire to change it.
Culture changes when the organization is transformed;
the culture reflects the realities of people working together every day."
Francis Hesselbein

DISCUSS – How does thinking about culture in terms of transformation rather than a program inform your thinking here? Where have you seen changes to your team or organization's culture since you began there? What precipitated the changes? What transformational process is necessary to see the systemic changes you'd like to see?

EXERCISE – Reflect on how boldness, bravery, courage, and the ability to carry on in spite of great odds are important traits for Bridge Building Leaders. What Bridge Building steps could you take this week to build strong, diverse relationships?

Bridge Building Leaders are first of all B.R.A.V.E. They are Brave, Resilient, Action oriented women who are cultivating their Voice and are in the process of Equipping and Expanding themselves and others to lead transformational change. And the good news is that these are all learned skills. In the next chapter we will explore the importance of resilience.

Developing Resilience

MARIE CURIE WAS THE FIRST FEMALE PROFESSOR at the University of Paris. Her contribution to physics had already been immense, illustrated by her two Nobel Prizes (1903 and 1911). However, her influence did not stop there. Her seminal work set the stage for subsequent generations of nuclear physicists and chemists. Marie's outstanding achievements included understanding the need to accumulate radioactive sources to treat illness and for research. She was also responsible for the creation of a theory of radioactivity (a term coined by her), techniques for isolating radioactive isotopes, and the discovery of two new elements, polonium and radium. One of my favourite quotes from this remarkable woman is: "Life is not easy for any of us. But what of that? We must have perseverance and above all confidence in ourselves. We must believe that we are gifted for something and that this thing must be attained."

Leaders get knocked around, misunderstood, disillusioned and discouraged. Setbacks are common. Progress takes longer than anticipated. Projects get cancelled. People betray. Calculated risks are necessasry. In order to build bridges BRAVE Women must embrace and develop the gift of resiliency.

In a 2010 TED Talk, Sheryl Sandberg—then COO of Facebook—encouraged women to sit at the table (not hold back) and keep our hand up (not give up).

She challenges us to not let our insecurity overcome our passion for our potential contribution.[123] Her talk is a clarion call to bravely speak up; to stand up; to not give up.

Examples of this kind of leadership abound. Ellen Johnson-Sirleaf, was the first woman ever elected president of an African country. Hers was not an easy path. Her commitment to democracy in Liberia led to her exile for many years. It was in this place of exile where she gained resilience. She also gained valuable leadership and international experience working for the World Bank and the UN. Her journey taught her to lead and overcome. Ellen, while a strong advocate of education, knew something that all great leaders know: "The biggest predictor of success is not IQ, it's resilience."[124] The willingness to take risks, to fail, to learn, to get up again, to take a new risk based on what you have learned, to fail again, to get up again… Indeed, the uncertainty and rate of change our world is experiencing is taking its toll on human beings. In response leaders need to become more and more resilient.

Merriam-Webster defines resilient as

> *: able to become strong, healthy, or successful again after something bad happens*
> *: able to return to an original shape after being pulled, stretched, pressed, bent, etc.*

Discuss – Which parts of this definition resonant with your experience of resiliency? What is the biggest and *best* failure you have ever experienced? What did it teach you? How have you learned to assess Return on Investment and take calculated risks?

Resilience is closely linked to hope. Without hope, it is difficult to get back up or to try again. Without hope, despair and disillusionment creep in, crowding out courage, inspiration, and compassion. The French general and emperor Napoléon Bonaparte, once wisely said, "a leader is a dealer in hope."

Reflect on this quote – Do you agree that one of the key attributes of effective, sustained leadership is the ability to inspire hope in oneself and others? In what ways is this true of your leadership?

FOUNDATIONS

HOW DOES OUR RESILIENCY DEVELOP? We can draw one important lesson from leadership studies and geology. In times of deep change and uncertainty, in times of genuine crisis, the bedrock we count on may feel more like shifting sand. When the rug is pulled out from under us—either by life circumstances, people's poor choices, or the systemic changes many people, organizations, and nations are facing—we look for purpose, as our bedrock.

I have always loved rocks and like many children brought home pockets full on a regular basis —my poor mother sometimes finding them when her old ringer washer literally ground to a halt as said pockets reached the ringer. It wasn't until I stood in an old graveyard, as part of an Environmental Studies undergrad program, measuring the effect of weather on those dated stones that I realized how much we humans count on rock. Not just to provide the ground we stand on—like the granite shield where I live, here in the Canadian north, or the ground rock beaches we call sandy and love to walk on, or the foundations of our homes and cathedral archways—but as the sturdiest thing we can think of on which to write the legacy of our loved ones. We count on rock to last.

You may recall from grade school that there are three main types of rock: igneous, sedimentary, metamorphic. Imagine the heat it takes to melt rock. Granite and obsidian are examples of igneous rock—both formed from molten lava melted deep below the surface.

Sedimentary rock, as its name suggests, forms when layer upon layer of sediment builds up over time and the pressure exerted as the weight from above and unmoving nature of the earth below literally crush the bits together. Talk about being between a rock and a hard place. Shale, sandstone and limestone are examples of this.

Shale then turns to slate and limestone turns to marble when caught between colliding tectonic plates and when the extreme heat and pressure combine to create the transforming process that leads to metamorphic rock.

Heat, Pressure, Time

- The kind of heat that we can only imagine as destructive
- The kind of pressure that would crush even the strongest human made barricade
- The kind of time that would make our times of waiting—no matter how lengthy or difficult—pale in comparison

Yet these very forces create the strongest and most valuable of substances. You may be thinking that heat, pressure, and time strengthen rocks but weaken people. Yet a year long study with thirty experts from eight countries[125] recently sought to codify the attributes that people who thrived during times of bedrock shifting uncertainty shared—and the factors and forces that built these attributes.

It turns out that the continuum of adult development that relates to how we think and process, also relates to how we manage change and how we will influence those around us during these times. They called this Vertical development. Horizontal Development describes the skills and knowledge we have—it could be measured by how full our cup is. Vertical Development seeks to discover how big the cup is and how to grow it bigger. Nelson Mandela, mentioned earlier, had the same information as many others of his day, yet he was able to make sense of this information, and therefore his world, in a wiser, deeper, more humane and more transformational way. And he was able to convince diverse partners and parties to join him in this counter intuitive bridge building. Ellen Johnson-Sirleaf, took the experiences of her exile and transformed them into fuel for her leadership.

Unfortunately, few people access this part of our ability. Fortunately, it is a mindset that can be learned. The research suggests that where we sit on the continuum is not based on our education, travels, or personality type—or at least not these alone. It is based on our experiences of:

Heat, Colliding Forces and the Right Kind of Support over Time[126]

Vertical Development

The very forces that we might only imagine as destructive, the kind of heat that shows up as challenges, failure, and uncertainty; the kind of pressure that arises from colliding worldviews that crush assumptions, expectations and dreams in its wake; and the kind of time that wearies us in waiting; these are the forces that create resiliency.

LIFE EXPERIENCE EXERCISE

Looking back over your life, what way-outside-your-comfort-zone *heat* experiences, colliding priorities and perspectives, and times of waiting have shaped and strengthened you? Diagram these experiences and insights as a timeline with both Vertical and Horizontal components.

LIFE EXPERIENCE EXERCISE

Recent breakthroughs in our understanding of our brain's neuroplasticity support the idea that both external experiences and our internal thought patterns not only change the way we think but also change the way we *can* think. We know that the brains of more resilient people show different levels of activity in different parts of the brain than those of less resilient people. Only recently have we learned that we can train our brains to be more resilient.[127]

Sisu

THE FINNISH WORD, *Sisu*, is said to capture the Finnish spirit. It means grit, determination, resilience, and bravery.[128] Not easily translated into English the word has almost mystical meaning. In Finnish literature and culture the word can be traced back hundreds of years. Its meaning goes far beyond physical or mental endurance to suggest an inner strength, a personal tenacity influenced by genes and life experience, but also developed through intentionality and the support of others. It refers to sustained courage, "spunk" and the ability to get back up after being knocked down. We use it here to describe that thing that you find when you dig deep and draw upon unknown resources to accomplish or overcome that which you previously thought impossible.

Resilience is the breakfast of change makers. As Mahatma Gandhi, leader of India's Independence Movement, once famously said, *"First they ignore you, then they laugh at you, then they fight you, then you win."*

BRAVE Women, Bridge Building Leaders quickly discover that resiliency is required to navigate the ever-changing landscape and inevitable pitfalls of their life work. Some of our falls will be big, painful, and public. Others will be small, private … and painful. Pain is the common denominator of falling. I have observed that the hardest obstacles are often the little, recurrent, demoralizing ones. The ones that gradually chip away at our resolve until we are not sure that we *want* to go on, let alone have what it takes to do so. Women rarely discuss these mini-obstacles and failures. They seem so petty compared to what others are facing. Yet, they can accumulate with devastating effect. Suddenly we are saying or doing something we truly regret and only in retrospect do we realize the fracture has been long in coming.

I remember the day I was speaking to a group of about one hundred and fifty people. It had been a rough week in the middle of a rough season of life and I was weary. That should have alerted me to use extra caution. Everyone knows that when we are hungry, angry, lonely or tired (HALT) our reserves get easily depleted and we are more likely to mess up. Everyone knows that except me, apparently. Just before standing to speak a friend engaged me in casual conversation. Venting to her set off a train wreck that somehow sideswiped my whole talk and soon I was publically sharing a story that I had not intended to share. It shamed a young woman I had been working with. Imagine my horror when I not only woke up to what I was saying but also looked out into the audience to see her and her friends sitting there. Needless to say, she left the room before I finished. It took me hours to find her so I could apologize. This may not seem like such a big thing. She was gracious and forgave me. Sadly, not one person chastised me or asked what was wrong. No one even seemed to notice. A few people even congratulated me on a great talk and a funny story well told. However, for me this was a devastating moment. With limited margin and unhealthy practices I had allowed minor things to become major and, in the process, become someone I did not want to be and had just hurt someone who did not deserve that kind of treatment. I was seriously disappointed in myself and have perhaps never been so strongly tempted to give up speaking and teaching. I did not know how I had gotten there or how to get to where I wanted to be.

RECALL A TIME when your "not best self" showed up. What did it show you about yourself? What did you learn from it and how has this helped to develop you both Vertically and Horizontally?

You may have seen the short clip from Gina Lollobrigida and Tony Curtis' 1956 movie "Trapeze" that someone has overdubbed to create a leadership metaphor. It is cheesy but I still love it. The actors soar through the air, letting go of one trapeze in an act of trust as they wait for the next to come within reach while a narrator relates that instant of panic and freedom to times of personal change. The message is clear. Only in these in-between spaces, when there is such a possibility of falling, is there also the possibility of flying.

TRAPEZE LEAP EXERCISE – Do you feel like you are between trapezes in any area of your life or work right now? Does it feels like you are falling or flying? Or is it possible that you are in training for the next leap? Or that you are holding too tightly to jump?

At the Leadership Studio, we work with many corporate for profit and not for profit leadership teams. Without fail they mention:

- Increased expectations and diminishing resources—both within and across departments—and within and across their organization and their partners and clients
- Changing demographics
- The complexity of building trust, community, and collaboration in an increasingly technologically dependent and geographically diverse era

Perhaps you are experiencing some or all of these realities. If so, you understand how important resilience is.

One of our most important initiatives in the Studio is a student leadership initiative we call the Resiliency program. Leadership development has been proven to increase self-efficacy, civic engagement, character development, academic success, and a number of other factors, making it an important piece of an overall success strategy for both youth and adults.[129] As kids begin to view themselves as agents of change, it alters the way they look at and respond to their world. It changes the way they look at themselves.

I hope and pray that these times are helpful for the students who come for retreats with us but I know for sure that few experiences have humbled me more, taught me more, or caused me to realize how sacred the ground is when we work with people.

In Industrial England, miners sent canaries down the shafts ahead of them to test the air quality knowing that these tiny birds were sensitive and would be more reliable indicators of healthy conditions than their own lungs. Many individuals and families, our current day canaries, are struggling—indicators of systemic societal overload. Voices to be listened to.

Each season our Public School, High School, Police, and Community Youth Work partners bring kids who are not thriving at school. Some come with challenges like English as a Second Language, bullying, substance abuse, physical or mental health struggles, and they often have the the kind of stressors at home that no child should ever have to navigate.

CHALLENGING REALITIES
(CONT'D)

One day we did a little exercise about the voice in our heads that stops us from being and doing all we could. During the exercise one young man, small and underdeveloped for his age, who we will call Chris, refused to share or participate. Hours later I sensed someone standing behind me, and turning, saw him pull from his pocket a rumpled paper with the words "my inner critic is my dad who says I am puny, useless, and should be dead" on it. He was 11-years-old. He held it out to me like an offering—allowing me for a second into the chaos of his world.

To acknowledge the realities of the kinds of knocks the world can send our way we use a simple exercise with students. We set a plastic bopper bag on the ground (the kind people purchase for small children to hit that have cartoon friendly words like "Sock" "Bop" or "Pow" on them). We explain that being healthy and strong does not mean a life with no 'knocks' but rather the ability to get back up after stumbling or being hit down. We just did this exercise last week. A young woman who had paid limited attention during our time together up to that point suddenly fixed her eyes on me as I said, "You may have discovered that life is not fair." That heavy stillness, indicating things could go really well or really wrong, descended on the group. I continued, "I wish it were otherwise but it is not. The people we most admire are people who have somehow found their way through this reality and been strengthened by it instead of weakened by resentment, despair, or skepticism." You could have heard a pin drop. "The question is how much power do you want to give to this unfairness and how much do you want to keep for yourself—to be and become the person you want to be in spite of it."

The next step of the exercise is to ask the kids to write on sticky notes the types of hypothetical or real things that mess with them and their day, with their sense of self. Some sticky notes are filled with lists—abuse, relationships at home, bullying, school, physical challenges, being on the spectrum, dependence on substances, self-hatred. Some are deceptively blank. The woman I mentioned above wrote, "my whole life."

Finally, we ask the students to fill a second sticky note with the things that strengthen them, help them to live into their true self, remember that they belong, and enable them to contribute. Many will write things like friends, music, someone who listens, sports, art, pets, hobbies, or being out in nature. Most admit that the number of items represented by the sticky notes at the top of the bag far outweigh those at the bottom that anchor them. Most agree that when things are going downhill it is less likely that we will have the resolve to build in additional strengthening relationships and practices. The time for this important work is now, before the next set of knocks occurs.

Of course, these inflatable punching bags are for kids. Are they really though? In the increasingly complex world of leadership, it is quite possible that there are uncertainties, challenges, and changes that are knocking you around too. If this is true, feel free to take a few minutes to complete the following exercise and then intentionally build more strengthening rituals, hobbies, relationships and moments into your life in anticipation of the strength you will need to positively face the unexpected set backs all leaders face.

BOPPER BAG EXERCISE

LIST ALL THE STRESSORS THAT TEND TO "KNOCK YOU AROUND." Add any you anticipate may be coming in the days ahead. Sit quietly with this list, acknowledging that this is a lot to carry. When ready, begin a second list outlining all the things that strengthen you—things like friends, family, music, hobbies, sports, exercise, faith or mindfulness, meaningful work, opportunities to use your strengths, food, fun, or being in nature. Make the list as long as you can. Now reflect on how many of these strengthening mindsets, relationships, and practices are part of your current reality. Are there any you need to more faithfully build in? Don't rush the process. Steep yourself in it until you feel ready to move on.

We have explored three metaphors that may be helpful in thinking about resilience so far.

* Trapezes require leaps and so does life
* Bopper Bags require a strong foundation and so do those who experience daily knocks
* Bedrock is transformed through heat, pressure and time... and so are the kind of people we call leaders, who can see the opportunity in times of deep change to gather diverse partners in the great work of genuine transformation

DISCUSS – Which metaphor resonates with you best?

INVARIABLY, THE AREAS THAT MOST INFLUENCE our ability to live and lead are deep and personal. They relate to our identity, our relationships, and our sense of purpose. Or, put another way, to our sense of belonging, being, and contributing. In 35 years of working with children, youth, and adults I have come to believe that these three are critical and that they are under attack. The following model, developed over many years and drawing from diverse interdisciplinary studies seeks to visually represent this. I call it the Thriving Model.

THRIVING MODEL:
BELONGING, BEING,
CONTRIBUTING

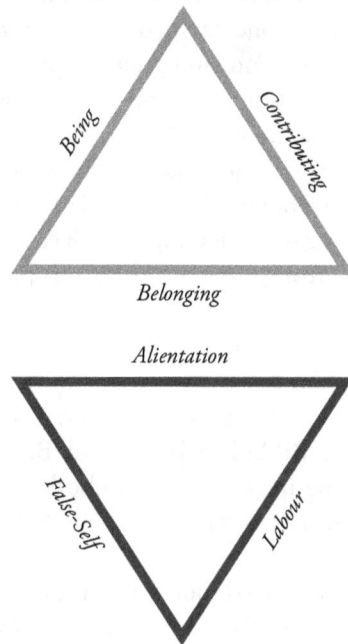

Figure 2. Thriving Model: Belonging, Being, and Contributing

The top triangle represents three key attributes that are crucial to thriving: Belonging, Being, and Contributing. The bottom triangle represents many people's opposite reality. BRAVE leaders collaborate to build bridges to flourishing lives and communities.

BELONGING, BEING,
CONTRIBUTING

BELONGING

THE BASE OF THIS MODEL IS BELONGING. I used to draw Being as foundational. Having embraced, "It is more important to be than to do" wisdom this seemed progressive. It wasn't until I engaged in more serious study of alternative worldviews that I realized how Western and narrow this thinking was. We have discussed how traditional African, Māori, and First People's worldviews highlight belonging as foundational. While one worldview is not necessarily more correct than another there are leadership insights to be learned by combining wise practices and exploring counter cultural premises. In many such cultures wellness includes physical, emotional, intellectual, and social components. Many Mediterranean and Arabic cultures share a strong value around family and hospitality to strangers. There is something powerful in this interdependent view that may resonate with you, as it does with me, although I do not pretend to have mastered its meaning or practice. For those not raised or naturally inclined to think this way it takes some consideration. Adrienne Clarkson wrote, "It is society that makes it possible for us to develop ourselves as human beings… we are all born biologically from a union. And it is as part of a group that we learn to belong."[130]

Much of our personal and social angst stems from a sense of alienation, a disconnection from our heritage and traditions as well as our extended families and neighbors. BRAVE Women and Bridge Building Leaders create places of belonging for themselves and others. We understand that without them we starve.

Inclusion trumps diversity.

A 2017 Culture Amp study asked thousands of respondents about diversity and inclusion. The findings take Rossabeth Moss Kanter's research notes earlier to the next level. Stated succinctly, "Diversity takes you from zero to one, while inclusion takes you from one to ten."[131] Inclusion trumps diversity. One factor stood out across all demographics—belonging. "I feel like I belong at my company" was the choice most correlated to workplace engagement in every subgroup.[132] The correlation was even more significant for those who are underrepresented numerically.[133]

This is significant. People who feel they belong perform better, become more willing to challenge themselves, and are more resilient.[134] While belonging may seem like a nebulous characteristic it can be both measured and developed. Office design, working hours and practices, face-to-face meetings that invite genuine participation, inclusive social events and mentoring programs where people can tell their story, and the absence of favoritism all build a sense of belonging. Subtle and even unconscious cues can also quickly undermine it.

BELONGING, BEING, CONTRIBUTING

BELONGING

INTERDEPENDENCE

DISCUSS – How intentional is your team/organization about building a sense of belonging?

We are all born dependent on a caregiver. Over time, most healthy people with sufficient resources and support (and often without them which is amazing when you think about it) develop a healthy sense of independence. In the West we value independence as an ultimate goal. Yet BRAVE women and Bridge Building Leaders understand that there is something beyond this stage. Something transformational. We call it interdependence. It includes the ability to give and take; to care for and be cared for, to love and be loved; to teach and to learn. We could draw this as a continuum and populate each segment in healthy ways.

DEPENDENCE _____ INDEPENDENCE _____ INTERDEPENDENCE

BELONGING, BEING,
CONTRIBUTING

BELONGING
INTERDEPENDENCE
(CONT'D)

Regardless of what your kindergarten teacher said, dependence is not always a sign of weakness. We are dependent on air, water and, quite frankly, lots of other people and things. Leaders who try to do it all themselves not only soon fail but have also totally missed an important component of Bridge Building. Dependence, as long as it is not co-dependence, is not necessarily bad.

Similarly, independence is a good thing. Every able woman with the chance should learn to fix, build, create, make decisions, plan, speak, and travel on her own. We do a great disservice to our girls if we teach them otherwise.

One of my favorite stories here involves a group of young women I had the privilege of working with. As part of a three-year long program they participated in an annual canoe trip. One year, the guide that joined them happened to be male. The trip was going well in spite of the inevitable challenges of a trip to the back woods with sixteen girls. Then one of the girls broke her flip-flop. They were the only shoes she had with her. Well, not broke so much as stepped so aggressively that the plastic piece that goes between your toes came out of the sole—making them impossible to wear, especially while portaging. She attempted to fix it for several minutes but was unsuccessful. Then, without thinking of the irony, on a girl's empowerment canoe trip as part of a girl's empowerment three-year long journey, she asked the one guy on the trip if he would fix it. Fortunately, this guy was stellar. Seeing the opportunity, he offered instead to loan her his pocket tool to see if that would help her to fix it herself. The group leader, my good friend Sophia, had the wisdom to see how important this incident was as a teachable moment. There was nothing wrong with this young girl asking for help. That is a sign of strength in my books. There is nothing wrong with her asking a guy to help. Again, it is a sign of strength to assess who is most skilled at a task. The challenge was that she had given up so quickly. This story has become metaphorical. A flip flop now hangs on the charm bracelets of each graduate of the program (alongside a BRAVE charm, a Tall Poppy charm to remind us we will not build our confidence by putting others down, and a Bee charm that symbolizes the skill of learning to "Float like a butterfly and, when necessary, Sting like a Bee."[135]). The story has been told and retold dozens of times since. And it always ends with this cheer, said with attitude, "I fix my own flipping flip flop."

So, dependence and independence are both good and important. Yet there is something magical that happens in the synergy of healthy interdependence. Across the past two decades the Search Institute and others have demonstrated that the number and intensity of high-quality relationships in a young person's life is linked to a broad range of positive outcomes.[136] Conversely, "[a]nxiety increases as social bonds weaken. Societies with low levels of social integration produce adults prone to anxiety." In fact, lack of social trust is the highest predictor of anxiety.[137] And here is the kicker… "The disruption of social ties disproportionately affects women and girls."[138] This makes sense doesn't it? We have discussed how important relationship-rich cultures are to women and girls. We have seen the breakdown of teams and societies when social ties deteriorate.

THE LEFT HAND SIDE OF THE THRIVING MODEL TRIANGLE represents our sense of self. Our identity. Our Being. The search for one's true self is a life long, deep, and empowering quest. It involves both outer experiences and inner reflection. Women with a strong sense of self are less intimidated by others, less likely to adapt themselves to fit in, less likely to need to stand out or hide away, yet more likely to speak up and stand up according to their values. They are also more likely to fess up when they make mistakes while not being devastated to discover they are not perfect. Women with a strong self of sense are more differentiated and emotionally healthy. These skill sets and mindsets are crucial to Bridge Building Leaders.

BELONGING, BEING, CONTRIBUTING

BEING

BELONGING, BEING,
CONTRIBUTING

BEING
(CONT'D)

CHOOSE ONE OR MORE THE FOLLOWING QUOTES to reflect on or discuss:

German poet, Rainer Maria Rilke once wrote:

*"Go into yourself and find out how deep is the place
from which your life springs."*

Polonius, in Shakespeare's powerful play Hamlet, sends off his son with the following well known words. *"To thine own self be true, and it must follow the day, the night. Thou canst be false to any[one]."*

Vince Lombardi, the legendary coach mentioned earlier, attributed his remarkable success to what he called the Lombardi Model. The model began with these words, "Only by knowing yourself can you become an effective leader."

The Greek philosopher, Socrates, (c. 470-399 B.C.) wrote "Be as you wish to seem."

"Be who you seem to be and seem to be who you really are."(Source unknown)

A sense of self includes knowing who *we* are. It is related to our sense of belonging. In fact, as we have seen, according to an Ubuntu perspective "I am because we are." This does not mean that a healthy sense of being is built on the *perception* of belonging—otherwise it crashes when we are no longer as popular or when we feel excluded. Belonging is more deeply rooted than acceptance into any group. In a world where people are besieged with distorted versions of acceptance, Bridge Building Leaders make room for who people really are and space for who they are becoming. This is deep work that begins with us. It should be treated as both sacred and unpredictable.

Some resources people find helpful in discovering more about themselves that are readily available include:

- DISC Personality Type Testing[139]
- MBTI Personality Type Testing[140]
- Values Assessments[141]
- Core Strengths Assessments[142]

Some people also find journaling, scrapbooking, or conversation around the following topics helpful. I have included a few areas you may want to reflect on below.

However, many people prefer the self-discovery found in community. Self-assessments that offer no opportunity for input from others may leave us with blind spots. It is difficult to truly know ourselves apart from community. Here again we see how foundational belonging is to our sense of self.

All that to say that if the assessments and reflection exercises are helpful, by all means use them. However if you happen to have a group of trusted people[143] who would be willing to invest two hours to hear your story, feedback the values and priorities they hear, and share the strengths and learning points they see in you this might be a richer experience for all involved. In fact, my experience has been that by the end of the two hours at least one or more people will ask for their turn the following week. If you

BELONGING, BEING,
CONTRIBUTING

BEING
A BLURRED LINE BETWEEN
BEING AND BELONGING

are really fortunate, this group of peers may turn into the peer learning and mentoring cohort you have been craving.

I have been fortunate in this. A consultant named Elaine Pountney led one of the most powerful planning sessions I have ever participated in. We were launching an international leadership development organization for women, and had so many pragmatic details to address, yet she spent the first several hours with us listening to our leadership stories. From these stories she helped us identify our leadership values, anticipate possible de-railers, and set both goals and boundaries. In the years since I have often used her strategy to help leaders unlock the wisdom hidden inside them. Several storytelling exercises are offered here for your use if they are helpful. They have often led to unexpected insights in the groups I have been a part of. As well as helping individuals, they also serve as powerful teambuilding exercises that can lead to increased team awareness and empathy.

"MY STORY" PICTURES EXERCISE – Choose three pictures from your family album if you can. One that shows you as a child and represents something that has always been important to you. One that shows you as a teen-ager and represents an area or time of angst you have experienced. One that shows you as an adult with people who matter to you. Describe why you chose each picture and what it means to you. Choose 3-7 words to summarize what you observe about each picture. Next, look for threads that tie the pictures together. Laying the pictures and summary statements about them on a large piece of paper begin to move them around until fresh insights jump out at you. Add these insights as well as any doodles, questions, thought bubbles, assumptions or arrows to the paper until you have created a piece that is helpful to you. Feel free to leave it for days at a time, revisiting it to see if any fresh insights pop out. What did you learn about yourself?

Step into the Circle exercise – This exercise is amazingly effective at breaking down walls and building affirmation and insight. Everyone stands in a circle around the person who is being affirmed. Those in the outer circle take turns telling stories that illustrate the greatest strength they believe the woman in the center brings to the team.

KEEP DOING, STOP DOING, START DOING EXERCISE – This targeted exercise requires a certain amount of trust so choose participants wisely and set some ground rules. It involves three rotations of input. In the first rotation—and the order is important—peers offer first-person input on what they appreciate that one member brings to the table. This is something they need or want you to keep doing in order for the team to be successful. In the second rotation peers dig a bit deeper (and you may feel a bit more vulnerable) as they share the observed behaviours[144] you may be unaware of that are making it harder for the team to function well. These don't have to be negative. They could be something like: "I need you to stop holding back when your opinion is asked for." Or it might be a bit more constructive like: "As an extrovert I need you to stop shutting down my external processing."

In the final round participants dig deeper still. Taking a deep and trusting breath we will hear the things the members of the group wish we would start doing. Some people dread this final round expecting unrealistic requirements yet are pleasantly surprised by the relatively minor adjustments that can make a huge difference to working relationships and effectiveness. Some common ones are: "I need you to start picking up the phone to call me rather than sending long or emotionally laden emails." "I wish you would set healthier boundaries for yourself so you can spend more time with your family, come to work more refreshed and we can learn from your modeling." "I'd love us to introduce some fun into our weekly meetings." Or, "I need you to clarify when a final decision has been made and outline what you need from me in light of it."

The third side of the model symbolizes our unique contribution. By this we mean our work —both paid and unpaid—as well as the signature attributes that we bring to any conversation or project. Many of these grow out of our being—our way of thinking and speaking, our core values and experiences. They may also grow out of our belonging—our upbringing, cultural norms, networks, role models, and mentors.

In Ancient Hebrew thinking, being, and doing could not be separated. In North America we think of them as two distinct things, often stressing to people that we should not define ourselves by what we do. For the Ancient Hebrew it made sense that what you do and say would flow out of who you are, and who you are is influenced by what you do.

Exercise – Consider the link between who you are (at your core) and what you do. How does one reflect and enhance the other?

Belonging, Being, Contributing

CONTRIBUTING

Visionary architect and thinker, Buckminster Fuller, when depressed and contemplating suicide is said to have asked himself the following two questions.

1. What is my job on the planet?
2. What is it that needs doing, that I know something about, that probably won't happen if I don't take responsibility for it?

REFLECT – What is my job on this planet? What is it that needs doing, that I know something about, that probably won't happen if I don't take responsibility for it?

The following Venn diagram demonstrates the sweet spot where Passion, Excellence and Need overlap. Having only two of the three pieces is not sufficient. Even if we are good at something, and others need and are willing to compensate us for it, we can burn out if we lack passion. Plenty of passion without skill can lead to failure. Perhaps most disappointing for many people is the scenario when we have the passion and the excellence for something that others do not want or are unwilling to compensate us for. In this case what we offer is undervalued by others and therefore undervalued by or unsustainable for us.

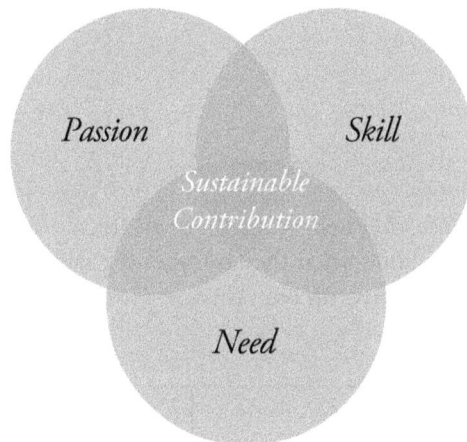

Skill + Need - Passion = Burnout
Need + Passion - Skill = Failure
Passion + Skill - Need = Devaluing

Figure 3. Sustainable Contribution

Of course, bringing value *through* our contribution is not the same thing as finding our value *in* our contribution. Healthy leaders know how to differentiate what can be motivating and life giving from what can be insidiously dangerous to others or self-destructive to us.

BELONGING, BEING,
CONTRIBUTING

CONTRIBUTING
UNIQUE CONTRIBUTION

Similarly, contributing is not the same thing as overachieving. Overachieving is one of the greatest distortions of our opportunity to make a difference in the world. In 2007, *The New York Times* published an article on high-achieving, ambitious girls and their "jam packed schedules," amped up multi-tasking and "profound anxiety." One mother expressed concern that the obsession with achievement could lead to "anorexia of the soul."[145] Beware of the obsession with achievement.

REFLECT – Many leaders struggle with finding our identity in our work or over-commitment. Is this an area of struggle for you? What have you done to wrestle it to the ground?

In contrast to those obsessed with, or unaware of, their contribution, healthy contributors know what they bring to the table. This is sometimes called our Unique Ability or our Unique Contribution and has been modeled like this:

UNIQUE ABILITY	EXCELLENCE
INCOMPETENCE	COMPETENCE

Figure 4. Unique Contribution (Source Unknown).

All of us have things that we are yucky at and, unless there is genuinely no one else there, would be better done by someone else. We all have things we can get by at. The things we are excellent at have taken time to develop. Since we have worked hard at them, we are often proud of or at least aware of them as strengths. Interestingly, they may or may not energize us just because we are really good at them if they lack interest or passion for us. We also have a few things, often things we have dismissed as unimportant or as something everyone can do, that represent what we uniquely bring to the table. This could be our ability to make people feel at ease, or to see the big picture, or to see the opportunity where everyone else sees problems. It could be our creativity or sense of humor or ability to turn chaos into order. It could be that people feel safer when we are around or that we are really good at building things or understanding complex theories or gauging how people are really doing. The point is that because it comes naturally to us, we may think it comes naturally to everyone. We tend to dismiss it and we are less likely to realize just how needed this attribute is.

To find it, we can look back into the toy box of our childhood to discover what we always loved to do and seemed to be born with. We can also listen to the things people commend us for that we tend to brush off as unimportant or obvious. Sometimes it is even helpful asking a few trusted friends, "If you were starting up a new company and wanted to hire me what would I bring to the team?" Be prepared for answers you were not expecting.

It is important to move as much of our time into the excellence and unique ability quadrants as possible if we want to truly lean into our ability to most fully contribute. The things we are excellent at we can teach because we know how we learned them. In fact this is the main thing Bridge Building Leaders do with the things that fall in this category—teach them to others. The things in the unique ability quadrant may be more difficult to teach because they come so naturally we don't know how we do them. These are the things we should not normally delegate to others. They are our Unique Contribution to the team.

Contributing according to our passions and unique ability rather than settling for aimlessness (lack of clarity about what to do), laziness (lack of motivation), work-aholism (working to prove or hide something from self and others) or being worked (coerced labor) is an important part of being human. Creating opportunities for others to contribute in this way is the work of Bridge Building Leaders! Consider the following exercise as a way to make space for the things that matter most.

Personal or Group Exercise – On a blank paper plate record randomly (on the flat surface) all the projects, responsibilities and significant relationships currently a part of your life. Do not stress about how many items to include or where to place them. Just add what comes to your mind knowing you can always add more later. Then take red, yellow, and green mini sticker dots and apply them beside each item to show which of these are draining you (red), giving you life (green) or neutral (yellow). Reflect on what you see. Are there any items that need to be delegated? Any things that must changed? Any things that are best accepted? Any relationships that need some work or need to be gently released? If there are significantly fewer green than red dots literally and metaphorically "on your plate" reflect deeply on why this is and if it is a necessary but temporary situation or something that can changed.

EXERCISE WITH TEAM – Draw the Venn diagram and Unique Ability (U.A.) charts on paper and moving around the group and inviting input from others discuss the sweet spot and U.A. you believe each person brings to the table. Use these insights to not only encourage your team but also assess that the right people are responsible for the right tasks.

Our own or someone else's unique contribution may look different than we expected. They may not show up as something we can touch or see. Sometimes they show up as suffering wrapped in insight.

Recently I met a young woman. Let's call her Karen. This young woman—grade 9—without emotion told her story of abuse, bullying, low self-esteem and struggles with her friends and her parents. She did not feel like she belonged. She did not think that becoming her true self was going to be enough. She could not see any way she was contributing to anything beyond her own and others' misery. I asked her who she was angry with and she named the usual—the bullies at school, her father, herself and then… tears finally sneaking through… God. At age 13 she was already shaken to the core—was nothing rock solid? Was no one or nothing trustworthy? Was there really no purpose to it all?

After sitting with her for several minutes I asked Karen to tell me about the people she most admired. Then I asked her if the lives of these people she admired had been easy. She said no. Opening my journal I read her one of my favorite quotes from Elizabeth Kubler Ros:

"The most beautiful people we have known are those who have known defeat, known suffering, known struggle, known loss, and have found a way out of the depths. These persons have an appreciation, a sensitivity, and an understanding of life that fills them with compassion, and a deep loving concern. Beautiful people do not just happen."

I promised her that even this part of her journey had meaning and that some day she would look back and see how it had both crafted and equipped her. She looked doubtful and I did not blame her. I remembered such days myself.

Reflect – How has suffering shaped the unique contribution you bring?

Resilience is developed through leveraging our strengths, discovering what strengthens us, finding meaning in the rough times, and by realizing we do not walk the path alone.

I LIVE IN THE NEAR NORTH. The following metaphor comes from the far north, from Inuit tradition and culture. From the piles of rocks called Inuksuk. In the Inuktitut language Inuk means "person," Inuit means "the people" and Inuksuk means "resembles people,"[146] or "to act in the capacity of a human."[147] There are many different kinds of these rugged rock structures. Those built in the shape of a person are called Inunnguaq. Used for communication and survival Inuksuk demonstrated a way of thinking that went beyond personal success to leaving markers so others could succeed as well. Traditionally these, sometimes massive, stone structures meant, "someone was here before you" or "you are on the right path." They were built to bring together the people who navigated over thousands of miles in far less than ideal conditions. Inuksuit were therefore closely linked to survival. Traditionally one to two meters tall these structures stood as literal and symbolic landmarks, lifelines and windows for travelers.[148] Inuksuit and Inunnguaq represent a worldview that celebrates strong ties to the land as well the strength of an individual balanced and supported by the community. They are considered sacred.

If we could have zoomed up to a bird's eye view of the Canadian north we would have seen thousands of these markers strategically placed across the vast landscape. Each one was both a silent message and a part of something much bigger than itself. Some of these stone markers stood as:

- Memorials to someone who had passed on
- Indicators of Resources
- Direction pointers
- North Star pointers so that even in 24 hour sun direction could be found
- Warnings alerting people to danger

However my favorite ones are those that spoke of:

- Presence. They were built purely so that the next traveler would know "You are not alone. I have been here before."
- Celebration. Suggesting there is joy in barren wilderness and it is worth remembering.

INUKSUK: WE ARE NOT ALONE

INUKSUK: WE ARE
NOT ALONE
(CONT'D)

Imagine now that you are like one of these rock formations, built over time into a marker that gives direction and support now and will leave that legacy long after you are gone. See that you are not alone in this—that there are thousands of other women, girls, men and boys around the world willing to stand up on behalf of others. Once you can visualize this concept attempt the next exercise.

PERSONAL OR TEAM EXERCISE – which Inuksuk do you represent? What role do you play for your family or team?

- Memorial – I honor what has gone on in the past
- Resources here – I compile and provide resources
- Direction pointer – I help people navigate
- North Star pointer – help people find their moral compass
- Warning – I alert people and our department/organization to danger
- Presence – You are not alone
- Celebrator – I help people find joy, even in the wilderness

DISCUSS – In what ways are Inuksuks a good metaphor for resilience?

EXERCISE – Reflect on how resiliency—the ability to get up when knocked around, the strength built through good times and hard times—is critical to Bridge Building Leaders.

Maria Corazon was the 11th President of the Philippines and is best known as the "Icon of Philippine Democracy." After her husband was assassinated, Aquino, with no prior political experience, became a unifying force in the opposition. Her presidency saw the restoration of democratic institutions and a renewed emphasis on civil liberties. However, her administration was not seamless. There were several military coup attempts. These partially derailed her attempts to build political and economic stability. In spite of this, she persevered, saying: "Faith is not simply a patience that passively suffers until the storm is past. Rather, it is a spirit that bears things—with resignation, yes, but above all, with blazing, serene hope."

DISCUSS – How does Maria Corazon Aquino's story speak to the role of hope and summarize many of the insights about resiliency and Bridge Building Leadership we have explored in this chapter?

Maria Corazon Aquino added advocacy and action to her bravery and resilience. In the next chapter we will see how we can do the same.

Advocacy and Action

IN ANCIENT HEBREW WRITING A LITERARY DEVICE was often used to draw attention to a central point—all things before it leading to it and all after supporting and adding to it. Using a modified version of this insightful method we have come to the tip of the arrow of the acronym BRAVE.

    Advocacy.
    Action.

Transformational dialogue and deed, replacing silence and suffering.

Drawn as an arrow it demonstrates:

- Bravery
  - Resilience
    - Advocacy and Action
  - Value and Voice
- Expanded Influence

For the ancient Hebrew words and actions were so closely linked that *word* could more accurately be translated *wordeed*. It was unthinkable that someone would say one thing and do another. It was understood that we speak loudly through our deeds. Drawing on this style of thinking we imagine advocacy and action as two sides of one coin. Two interchangeable parts. Two tools in the tool belt of BRAVE Bridge Builders.

Merriam-Webster defines an advocate as a person who argues for or supports a cause or policy; a person who works for a cause or group; a person who argues for the cause of another person in a court of law.

No wonder we often think of an advocate as someone who speaks or acts on behalf of someone who cannot. While this definition may be helpful, and true in some cases, it is equally untrue and unhelpful in many others. Especially when it reflects a paternalistic approach. Intervention, from the Latin for "to come between, to interrupt" must be approached with great care lest we come between and interrupt, more than intended.

It is generally wiser to think of advocacy as coming alongside others to hear their story and, where appropriate, support their priorities or processes. Otherwise, even with the best of intentions, we can set up patterns whereby people feel disempowered and dependent rather than empowered and encouraged. This phenomenon is sometimes referred to as "Learned Helplessness" and is the antithesis of the true work of an Advocate. Not to mention it is disrespectful to not allow people to speak for themselves what they believe and need.

"To lead people, walk beside them."
Lao-tsu, Chinese philosopher
(c. 4th-6th century BC)

To be an advocate for others is first and foremost to think deeply about what it means to be human. Interestingly, many people groups' original names mean "the people" or "the humans." The people who were once called the "Auca" by others—meaning "savage"—used the name *Wao* for themselves, meaning "human." Prior to the arrival of the Spanish, the people we now call the Navaho, called themselves *Diné*—meaning "human."[149] *Inuit*, the name chosen by the people of Canada's far north, means "the people." As human beings we share so many similarities including the need for dignity and choice.

DISCUSS – Although this may seem like a purely philosophical exercise I encourage you to think deeply about this before moving on. What does it mean to be human?

*"Each mind is a
different world."*
Mexican proverb

We share so much in common. In fact, scientists believe that across all people groups we share between 99 and 99.9% of our DNA.[150] Yet, at the risk of stating the obvious, we are also more culturally and personally diverse than we might at first imagine. Seeing the world through such different lenses, we therefore see different things as important, right, good, fair or just. BRAVE Bridge Building Leaders understand and embrace this by valuing diversity, creating inclusive cultures and intentionally challenging and expanding their own worldview.

We will explore this in more detail in the final chapter but for now, lets consider how it impacts advocacy and action.

ADVOCACY AND
TRANSFORMATION

ADVOCACY IS A POWERFUL THING. BRAVE leaders use it in two transformational ways.

1. To advocate with and for others, not just in the "speaking up for those who cannot speak for themselves" kind of way we have come to think of advocacy, but as something much deeper, more challenging, more lasting and more transformational.

2. To advocate for ourselves. Not in a "these are my rights" kind of way, but rather coming to the table with a thoughtfully considered opinion in one hand ready to be offered and a second, open, hand ready to receive and learn from other perspectives.

Advocacy and social action are important—but pursuing them is fraught with danger. It may seem odd to stress the dangers of advocacy and social action in a chapter dedicated to promoting it. Consider, however, how much damage has been done in the name of progress, capitalism and religion. In exploring these—and their opposites—we will hopefully approach more humbly and wisely the complex issues our world faces and the people most impacted by them.

THERE ARE AT LEAST NINE GRAVE DANGERS when it comes to advocacy and social action.

The first is complacency. The antithesis of complacency is not compassion, for tears are not enough. The antithesis to complacency is immersion —immersing yourself in the world and getting to know the people (or animals or whatever you are wanting to understand better) and places, that transform a cause into a relationship.

Complacency should not be confused with margin—our second grave danger. Complacency suggests we don't know enough to care enough to do something. Margin suggests we care but cannot imagine adding one more thing into our lives. In my experience margin is the number one perceived deterrent to many caring people. As we reflect together we may begin to discover previously hidden ways that we are already advocating and acting, as well as ways we can leverage these opportunities with more intentionality. Our goal is balance not burnout. Reassessing margin involves de-cluttering our lives so as to make space for those things that are most important. Our aim is powerful advocacy and action rather than guilt driven (or even well intentioned but misguided) chatter and busyness. Advocacy and resiliency are closely linked. In fact persistence, resiliency and rest are inseparable sisters.

The third danger when it comes to advocacy and justice seeking is good deeds done to make ourselves look or feel good and its close cousin, the danger of feeding someone else's family when our own are in need of our time.

A fourth danger is compassion without focus.

In a world with so many needs it can be difficult to know where we best fit in. When it comes to unearthing our passion I suggest that we think like detectives—looking for MOTIVE, MEANS and OPPORTUNITY.

ASK – What is your MOTIVE for addressing this issue? How has it influenced you? For example, many people dedicate their lives to science or medicine after seeing a loved one pass away from illness that research or treatment might have prevented or cured.

ASK – What MEANS do you have at your disposal? Time, resources, expertise? How might they best be used?

ASK – What OPPORTUNITIES are within your reach? A neighborhood school seeking adults to read to kindergarten students? A nursing home with lonely clients? A fundraiser in your community hall this Friday? A friend already involved in something worthwhile that you could support? A global issue you could investigate on your next business trip or leverage your organization's resources to address?

LIST what you are passionate about here:

LIST hobbies or interests that are important to you:

FREEDOM COMES
AT A COST

WHEN DELVING MORE DEEPLY into what we are passionate about, self-awareness as well as others' insights can guide us. I have noticed that what others may call overly sensitive or even negative behaviour can sometimes give us great clues. As we dig into the roots of our thinking we often find powerful motivators that can be leveraged in dynamic ways. Do you value autonomy so highly that it irks you more than most when you are micromanaged? Perhaps freedom is a cause you could really get behind. This could take the form of joining a movement to end human trafficking, or researching what companies to avoid purchasing from because of their labor practices.

Freedom comes at a cost. The stories of Viola Desmond, Rosa Parks, Gandhi, Martin Luther King Jr. and Nelson Mandela demonstrate this. Not all of us will have the calling or constitution to follow closely in their footsteps but all BRAVE Bridge Builders must fight for the value of freedom. For, make no mistake, fear (and its unlikely cousin complacency) bring a much higher cost than freedom. It only takes one tyrannical leader, one oppressive system, one more turning of a blind eye... some things are worth fighting for.

Martin Luther King Jr. went to jail rather than pay a fine. Writing from his Birmingham jail cell, he said, "Injustice must be exposed, with all the tension its exposure creates, to the light of human conscience and the air of national opinion before it can be cured." Some freedoms are worth fighting for.

Freedom is both internal and external. The internal chains can be stronger than the external. Otherwise why would many women, released from the sex trade return of their own volition. Many slaves and convicts take years to learn to live as free people. BRAVE Bridge Builders understand the road to freedom is long and complex.

One final note about freedom: Oppression has a nasty way of repeating. Abused become abusers, oppressed become oppressors. BRAVE Bridge Building leaders understand that freedom has not been won until this cycle is broken. Game changing BRAVE Bridge Builders understand that true freedom is not won until both the oppressed and the oppressor have been truly set free… and—in the spirit of Nelson Mandela's vision for South Africa, some models of restorative practice, and Truth and Reconciliation dialogues—miraculously reconciled.

ASK – How high a value is freedom to me? If I were to liberate this latent potential in life-giving ways what might it look like?

Do you find yourself saying, "that is not fair" a lot and questioning why things are the way they are? Perhaps justice is a value worth you fighting for. This could take many forms: addressing kids arriving without breakfast in your local school; ensuring everyone has equal access to education or fair wages for work done; making sure everyone's voice is heard around the table; writing a letter in your local paper about unfair practices; or any number of small or big decisions you personally make.

Justice is often defined as: the process or result of using laws to fairly judge and punish crimes (judgment); the quality of being impartial or fair (righteousness); conformity to truth, fact or reason (correctness).

WHEN THINKING OF SOCIAL JUSTICE we expand this definition beyond laws and punishment to consider people's unmet needs. This enables us to move from "who did what wrong?" to how can we right the wrongs of our world? And ultimately how can we create the kind of environment in which people can thrive? The work of Ancient Hebrew judges and many Ancient First Nation elders was not only to determine and protect someone's rights—as important as that might be. Their role was, where possible, working to restore or "make right" the relationships between the two parties. They were concerned with the overall health and well being of both the victim and the perpetrator, as well the spiritual relationship of both parties to their Creator and the world at large.

JUSTICE AS A MINDSET

JUSTICE AS A MINDSET
(CONT'D)

ASK – How does this view of justice, and the role of judges, influence your view of advocacy? What might an ethic of flourishing look like when it comes to issues of Social Justice?

Yet even with this expanded view there is so much room for paradox and disagreement. While even young children have an innate sense of justice, what seems like an injustice to one person may not to another. Or, some will see gradations where others see blatant violations. Or, we may agree that something is unjust but disagree about what needs to be done about it.

How then can we think about ourselves as advocates for justice? Some people will accompany others to courtrooms and lend their courage to those who have difficult opponents to face. Others may speak up against bullying or build bridges between groups who have lots and groups who have less. Others will wake up to the injustices in their neighborhood and take a stand against racism, age-ism, sexism, domestic violence, or date rape. Others will lobby local governments or join a soup kitchen. Others will choose careers in order to make a difference in this area. Economists, politicians, judges, educators, parents, business people, law enforcement agencies, religious leaders, farmers, scientists, and many other types of people are needed for the important work of the just allocation of respect, freedoms, power, responsibility, resources, and opportunities.

All BRAVE Bridge builders can explore how selfishness, greed and entitlement are—perhaps unknowingly—influencing us. How my purchasing is affecting child laborers half way around the world, how my over-consumption is contributing to the depletion of resources, my preference for fresh strawberries out of season is adding to our carbon footprint...my...my...my...

You may have seen the TV ad featuring a little girl surrounded by her toys saying, "Everything you see before me is mine." While entertaining the message is also disturbing. The craving for possession and the trap of entitlement start early… mine… mine… mine…

The sooner we acknowledge this the better. However, do not let guilt and regret trap you further. If you are one of the fortunate who rises each morning without fear of starvation or threat of violence practice the following:

- The opposite of greed is generosity—even a small act can have huge impact.
- The opposite of selfishness is kindness—it never ceases to amaze me how kindness leads to breakthrough.
- The opposite of entitlement is thankfulness—make noticing and appreciating the little things a daily practice.
- The opposite of injustice is dignity and respect—justice is always personal.
- And perhaps most importantly, the opposite of denial is awareness—read the paper, visit neighborhoods that are different from your own, observe your own patterns of thought and behavior. We do not need to wallow in what is wrong with the world but, surrounded by people who think about and experience the world in ways similar to ours, we easily slip into group think, self justification and compromise.

You can see how we have moved beyond "that is not fair to me" to a mindset that is attuned to creating a more just world. We have entered the world of ethical thinking and creating environments where people can thrive rather than, at best, survive. We have entered the world of restoration and transformation—the world every Bridge Building leader chooses to live in. This does not necessarily mean switching vocations. This is about becoming more aware of why we are the way we are, more intentional about using the opportunities before us and realizing that we cannot leave this for someone else to do because they may not see it as clearly as we do.

JUSTICE AS A MINDSET
(CONT'D)

We often think of justice as an act but it could equally be considered a mindset. I love this way of thinking about it, "Justice is to be measured by the extent to which people honor their obligations to live in relationships that uphold the equal dignity and rights of the other."[151]

GROUP DISCUSSION – Martin Luther King, Jr. once famously said, "the universe is on the side of justice." Do you agree? What do you think he meant by this?

Perhaps you are the kind of person who hates conflict. You may have been called conflict avoidant and been asked to participate in assertiveness training classes. Or, maybe peace is a high value that you cannot help craving and creating everywhere you go. Peace is defined as: a state in which there is no war or fighting; harmony in personal relations; freedom from disquieting or oppressive thoughts or emotions.

Many traditions around the world share this value. Ancient Hebrews called it *Shalom*, a word that is difficult to translate into English as it encompasses our idea of peace as well as other nuanced meanings like wholeness, well being, health, prosperity, balance, and completion. Māori people use the word *Hauora* to convey the personal and community wellbeing that incorporates four dimensions of wellbeing: physical, emotional, spiritual, and social.

How can we think about ourselves as Advocates for Peace? Some people practice Passivism or lobby against war. Others may provide respite so that parents of high-needs children can have a break, or foster children so that kids from stressful backgrounds have a period of peace in which to discover that life can look differently. The point is that everyone can do something and for some people this may be a big part of the reason they are on this earth. Peacekeeping can be as simple as choosing to stop a rumor or pausing to truly consider someone else's position… and it can be as life changing as a career choice or a decisive stand.

Conflict affects us personally, relationally, structurally, and culturally. Of course, some amount of conflict is normal and even healthy. In fact to envision peace as a "static end state"[152] is to misunderstand the dynamic and relational nature of human interaction. Peace is rooted in the ever-changing quality of relationships and context. Some would argue that even the language—Conflict Resolution—is unhelpful and that Conflict Transformation is a better end goal. Resolution suggests the end to something undesirable, which, while appealing may also be more fleeting. Transformation asks, "How can we end something not desirable while building something we do desire?" "A Transformational view engages two paradoxes as the place where action is pursued and raises three questions: How do we address conflict in ways that reduce violence and increase justice in human relationships? How do we develop a capacity for direct, face-to-face interaction and, at the same time, address systemic and structural changes? …[How do we minimize] conflict through non-violent approaches which address issues and increase understanding, equality and respect in relationships"[153] amongst individuals, groups or societal structures who do not see eye to eye? Enter those BRAVE enough to be Bridge Building Leaders.

PERSONAL OR GROUP DISCUSSION – In what ways are you actively involved in Peace Keeping (but may not have seen it that way before)? In what ways would you like to be more involved?

JUSTICE AS A MINDSET
(CONT'D)

Perhaps you are more likely than others to notice someone who has not spoken up in a meeting and find a way to invite them in? If so, might inclusiveness be a high value for you? People with this value understand better than most that exclusivity impacts not only those left out but the richness of the community itself. They understand that such behaviour is an indicator of a systemic imbalance that, left unchecked, can develop into dictator-like approaches to progress. Imagine what our world may be missing if you get this but have not yet found a way to effectively speak this truth into your sphere of influence?

DISCUSS the following concept: Mahatma Gandhi once said, "The true measure of any society [or community] can be found in how it treats its most vulnerable members." Do you agree? Disagree? How do you see this principle working out in your community?

Do you sometimes annoy people by telling them more truth than they were expecting? Maybe truth is important to you…You get the point… dig into why you notice or react to things others don't and you may discover not only why but also how to multiply the positive impact one hundred fold.

REFLECT – What deep values or motivators do you see at work in your life? How have you leveraged these in Bridge Building ways? Has this conversation sparked an interest to dig deeper or explore ways to more proactively contribute to something bigger than your self? What would be the first step towards this?

Where passion and pain collide is where our calling is often found. BRAVE Bridge builders learn to leverage the pain and interruptions of our lives. Phan Thi Kim Phúc's story illustrates this powerfully. This Vietnamese-Canadian woman is best known as the child subject of a Pulitzer Prize winning photograph taken during the Vietnam War on June 8th, 1972. The iconic photo shows her at about age nine running naked on the street after being severely burned by a South Vietnamese napalm attack. It took seventeen operations and a long journey of outer and inner recovery to save Kim's life. Throughout this time she grew determined to become a doctor. However her studies were continually interrupted by officials desiring to use her story for propaganda purposes. She and her husband later defected to Canada. "It seemed that picture didn't want to let me go. At first, I was very upset. And then a wonderful thing happened. I thought, 'If I can't escape that picture, I can work with it for peace.' I accepted it as a powerful gift for me."[154] Bridge Building Leaders utilize everything at their disposal, even their pain, and understand that the longings they have may be mere inklings of something even deeper.

REFLECT – How has suffering shaped the unique contribution you bring?

Our contributions may look different than we expected. They may not show up as something we can touch or see. Sometimes they show up as suffering cradling insight. Sometimes they take years to emerge. Other times they appear as a tiny seedling, so fragile we doubt their ability to influence. Yet, speaking now as a grandmother, I promise you these unlikely appearances often have the most meaning of all.

A fifth danger rises naturally from idealism, mixed with the desire for personal satisfaction and immediate gratification. This may take many forms.

The belief that we can overcome complex issues with a single strategy or short-term fix.

The desire to build a new organization rather than partner with those already working in the area.

Unable to exist for long in the tension between what we have and what we long to see, BRAVE Bridge Builders may be tempted to settle for a lesser vision, pulling back on the dream in order to see if it can be accomplished more quickly or easily.

Alternatively, we may strive for perfection, refusing to accept good enough when good enough truly is good enough.

Or we may insist on it looking the way we envisioned when we started, forgetting most visions develop as new insights are gleaned along the way. One antidote to this danger is to think like a rock climber. A rock climber sees the immensity of the mountain to be scaled. They plot a course, ask those who have gone before, read the weather, then they prepare, over prepare and prepare for every contingency. Even with this level of intentionality and care, the rock climber knows there will be times when they need to go sideways to find a better hold or backwards to re-assess a different route. Even with this level of intentionality and care, the rock climber counts on their team to get them through and commits to being there for their team when things get tough. BRAVE Bridge builders approach their work with a similar mix of zeal and openness.

A sixth danger lies in tying our identity too tightly to our contribution. Again, believing that we bring value through our contribution is not the same thing as believing our value is found in our contribution. Similarly, contributing is not the same thing as overachieving. Overachieving is one of the greatest distortions of our opportunity to make a positive difference in the world.

The seventh, and perhaps most challenging, danger comes from assuming we can solve issues that we have not lived or truly learned. BRAVE Bridge Builders are cautious about giving advice where we have no credibility, or speaking for someone when we should support the process that will enable them to speak for themselves.

Te tīmatanga o te mātauranga ko te wahangū,
te wāhanga tuarua ko te whakarongo.
The first stage of learning is silence
The second stage is listening.
Māori Proverb

Ellen Johnson-Sirleaf, who we mentioned earlier, understood the importance of helping people become their own advocates. She once famously said, "The people of Liberia know that government cannot save the country—only their own strength, their determination, their creativity, resilience and their faith can do that." This perspective did not eliminate the government's responsibility but it did change its focus. Ellen saw her role as building the bridges that would enable the people to save their own country. Bridge Building Leaders rarely build the bridge alone. They act and advocate so that others can shape and share in the journey.

In fact, Bridge Building Leaders invite those most affected into the heart of the process. Marian Anderson, one of the most celebrated singers of the twentieth-century and an important figure in the struggle for African-American artists to overcome racial prejudice in the United States once said: "Leadership should be born out of the understanding of the needs of those who would be affected by it."

Several years ago, I was leading a strategic planning session with a group of friends in Russia. They just didn't seem to be "getting it." I struggled on, wondering if it was a translation issue, if my visuals were not helpful, if we all needed more coffee or just what was going wrong. Then one brave participant explained that the whole premise upon which my model was designed was not only foreign but also unhelpful in their context. The issue was far deeper than I had realized and surfaced my own limited perspective. The authors of the Globe Study—a massive research project that examines Culture, Leadership and Organizations across sixty-two societies—write, "Leadership is culturally contingent…views of the importance and value of leadership vary across cultures."[155] An important aspect of the study was the extent of alignment across cultures of actions and characteristics endorsed as contributing to effective leadership. Twenty-one attributes or behaviours were universally identified as contributing to leadership effectiveness. Eight were universally identified as impediments. And thirty-five were seen as contributors in some cultures and impediments in others.[156] What was valued in leaders in one culture was seen as detrimental in another in over half the attributes and behaviours assessed. Now that is thought-provoking and humbling. Bridge Building Leaders must be intentional in developing cultural literacy.

BRAVE Bridge Building Leaders also understand that each journey will be unique. Indira Gandhi was the first female prime minister of India. She grew up in an intensely political atmosphere, attended Oxford University and became involved in the movement for Indian Independence. In the 1950s, she unofficially assisted her father as the first prime minister of India. Indira won both elections and the hearts of the people. She introduced more liberal economic policies and promoted agricultural productivity. During a period of great hardship and upheaval she led wisely and well. She also understood that her role included encouraging her country to greatness by finding its own way. She once said: "A nation's strength ultimately consists in what it can do on its own, and not in what it can borrow from others."

Indeed, BRAVE Bridge Building Leaders often need to find untested, unconventional, or fringe methods in order to see the kinds of breakthroughs they desire. Florence Nightingale was a pioneering English nurse, writer, teacher, and statistician. During the Crimean war she and others were instrumental in changing the role and perception of nursing, as well as significantly improving the treatment of wounded soldiers. So effective were their techniques that some suggest that within 6 months of their arrival in modern day Istanbul, the mortality rate among British soldiers dropped from 42 percent to 2.2 percent. Florence is a brilliant example of someone who challenged conventional perceptions and methods... and radically influenced her world as a result. Bridge Building Leaders may even need to step outside the rules of the social norms of their culture—often at a personal cost. Florence once said "And so is the world put back by the death of every one who has to sacrifice the development of his or her peculiar gifts (which were meant, not for selfish gratification, but for the improvement of that world) to conventionality."

Discuss – In what ways have you had to break with convention in order to see the change you wanted to see? Is there something you are currently working on or concerned about that may require a fresh approach?

Breaking convention may not mean developing something new. It may mean returning to ancient ways. As we will see over and over throughout this book, women who can tap into their personal heritage are better prepared to access it in pursuit of a better future. 150 years after Florence, Josephine Mandamin set out to walk the thousands of miles around the Canadian Great Lakes to highlight their environmental collapse. As an Anishinabe elder from Thunder Bay, Canada she knew that in the Anishinabe tradition, as in many traditions around the world, women fetch the water. So, in 2003, when Josephine Mandamin was "moved" to speak out for the Great Lakes, she decided to circle the lakes and tell people "the water is sick... and people need to really fight for that water, to speak for that water, to love that water." At every tributary, Josephine stopped to talk directly to the water, offer prayers, tobacco, and thanks. "I've heard so many times, 'You're crazy,'" she says. "But we know it's not a crazy thing we're doing; we know it's for the betterment of the next generations." Each year since Josephine, co-founder of Mother Earth Water Walks continued to trace the lakes and rivers of Canada's Great Lakes river system. By 2014 she had walked almost 11,000 miles with a copper pail of water in one hand and a staff in the other.[157] Her words are as telling as her actions, "I will go to any lengths to carry the water to the people."[158] In classic BRAVE Bridge Building Leadership style Josephine Mandamine also got 100 First Nation communities to sign the First Nations Great Lakes Water Accord and tirelessly works to improve dialogue between the Anishinabek and the Government of Canada. She also mentors youth, dialogues with interested businesses, organizations and individuals, and invites others into the journey. In recognition of her work Josephine received a 2015 Lieutenant Governor's Ontario Heritage Award.

Advocates also know to look to different cultures to learn practices that are powerful and sustainable while being aware of the dangers of cultural appropriation. In ancient Māori culture important discussions came to a *whare*, a Meeting House, where everyone was given the opportunity to speak, to say their truth, to tell their story.[159]

REFLECT – When was the last time you were in this kind of group environment? What happened? When was the last time you created this kind of environment for others? What might this look like in your context?

DISCUSS – How do you respond to these stories? Which one(s) most resonate with you? Why? How do you envision the responsibility of leaders when it comes it to action and advocacy motivated by social conscience? What application can you draw for your own context?

Positive Deviance

Bridge Building Leaders consider alternatives as well as diverse approaches. One such example is called Positive Deviance.[160] This model highlights those who are facing the same challenges and functioning within the same constraints as others yet are highly successful because of having adopted practices that are outside the norm. The approach represents the antithesis of bringing in experts or best practices used elsewhere. It is deceptively simple in concept yet difficult to execute. The first step involves discovering those in a community whose approach, often grass roots and often against the norm is—against all odds—actually working. The second step involves uncovering the practices they are using and allowing these innovators—who have great credibility—to influence their own peers.

Positive Deviance has been used in dozens of countries for hundreds of diverse applications and as a hands on, solution based approach has been attributed to:[161]

- a 30-50% reduction in childhood malnutrition across forty-one countries worldwide,
- a 30-62 % reduction in transmissions of antibiotic resistant bacteria in three US hospitals, and in the process, a bridging of the status divide in hospital hierarchies,
- a dramatic reduction in neonatal mortality in Pakistan, along with a blurring of defined gender roles and an increased voice for women
- a 50% increase in primary school retention in participating schools in one province in Argentina as well as reduced social barriers between teachers and illiterate parents
- a 30% reduction in girl trafficking in poor villages in East Java through the vigilance of the entire community

Amazingly, the solutions often turn out to be remarkably simple and sustainable. However, while the specific practices and tools are important, the authors argue that "the particular journey that each community must engage in to mobilize itself, overcome resignation and fatalism, discover its latent wisdom and put this wisdom into practice" is far more critical.[162]

The approach is not applicable in every situation but is worth considering for addressing problems that:

1. Are enmeshed in a complex social system
2. Require social and behavioural change
3. Entail solutions that are rife with unforeseeable or unintended consequences[163]

BRAVE Bridge Builders also know they cannot do everything. Choosing what not to do is an important skill and discipline. One strategy to help us discern this is separating that which is sustainable and life giving from that which drains us.

PERSONAL OR GROUP EXERCISE – Revisit the paper plate exercise from page 94. Add any additional projects, responsibilities, and significant relationships that you may have thought of since then. You can always go back and add more. Review items that are draining you (red), giving you life (green) or neutral (yellow). Reflect on what you see. What portion of your energy are you spending on your unique contribution? What portion are you spending on your sustainable contribution, where passion, skill, and need meet? Do either of these need adjusting? Reflect on the items that are draining you (red dots). Are they important enough to you personally to keep doing? Who can support you in through necessary but draining activities? What buffers can you build in to support yourself?

INHERENT DIGNITY

HOW THEN DO WE DECIDE WHAT IS GOOD AND FAIR AND JUST? Many people would agree with former President of the Philippines and practicing economist, Maria Gloria Macapagal-Arroyo's desire: "I want justice to be so pervasive that it will be taken for granted, just as injustice is taken for granted today." The quintessential question is how do we get to this place without assuming we know best and repeating the horrors of colonization?

The United Nations Universal Declaration of Human Rights begins, "Whereas recognition of the inherent dignity and of the equal and inalienable rights of all members of the human family is the foundation of freedom, justice and peace in the world, Whereas disregard and contempt for human rights have resulted in barbarous acts which have outraged the conscience of mankind, and the advent of a world in which human beings shall enjoy freedom of speech and belief and freedom from fear and want, has been proclaimed as the highest aspiration of the common people"[164] and then goes on to outline 30 articles by which human rights should be protected.

"The words of the elders do not lock all the doors; they leave the right door open."
Zambian Proverb

Advocacy is closely linked to character and values. Yet it is dangerous to assume that someone not sharing our values lacks character. In any group of people many life-giving values will be represented. If each of us were to champion each one, we would soon become overwhelmed. However, when a culture permits all its members to speak up about the values that matter most to them we are all made aware of our blind spots, unwise practices, and even prejudices.

We live in a beautiful yet broken world. A world in need of thousands upon thousands of BRAVE Leaders. How can it be that so many bright, well-connected and committed people have not been able to wrestle some of the huge challenges and injustices of our world to the ground? How is it that in this generation:

- 80% of the world lives on less than $10 per day; more than 20% on less than $1.25. Hunger is the number one cause of death in the world—22,000 children dying of poverty every day. 750 million people are without adequate access to clean, safe drinking water.[165]
- Estimated numbers of people caught in Human Trafficking range from 20 to 32 million people—as much as the population of Canada. And in Canada, as in many parts of the world, 25% of those trafficked are minors. Even more startling is the fact that 50% of victims are aged 18-24 and so are 41% of perpetrators.[166]
- At our current rate of consumption and waste, primarily in the West, we need 1.666 planets to sustain our existing population.[167] More than 800 animals (that we know of) are extinct and another 19,000 are endangered or vulnerable.[168]
- Worldwide, 35% of women will endure some form of violence.[169]
- While the number of armed conflicts appears to be deceasing, the number of deaths from each conflict is escalating. Meanwhile, the world spends just $1 on conflict prevention for every $1,885 it spends on military budgets.[170]

…Not to mention worldwide issues of neglect, loneliness, mental and physical illness, overcrowded prisons, racism, loss and grief, elder abuse, breakdown of families and communities, political unrest, addictions, and bullying…

We are going to need more creativity, more diversity of thinking, more inclusivity and collaboration, and more Bridge Building. We are going to need all of us to speak up. Bridge Building Activists and Advocates understand the power of developing a Voice that is rooted in our Values.

Cultivating Voice

The human voice is the organ of the soul.
Henry Wadsworth Longfellow

VOICE TRANSCENDS SPOKEN WORD. It grows from a place deep within us and informs not only our private and public conversation and but also our priorities and practices.

You may have heard the old adage "Walk softly and carry a big stick." The origin of this saying is said to go back to a letter Theodore Roosevelt wrote in 1900. It refers to the practice of balancing diplomacy and power. We use it here to address a common challenge many people encounter when discovering their voice: finding the right tone. For ironically, defensiveness makes it more likely that we will be dismissed. As we have noted previously, when an individual or group has been held back or kept down, one can anticipate they will eventually come roaring out with a vengeance. This is completely understandable. The life-long abuse many people have endured—not to mention the centuries-long pain many people groups have experienced—will not normally be something they can talk about without emotion, resentment, anger, and even hatred. Yet sadly this natural response may detract from others' ability to truly hear the message. I remember when I first started speaking and teaching about women's issues.

In one workshop, filled mainly by men, I was being particularly careful to be rational and educational rather than reactionary. I therefore responded with great surprise when one of the participants thanked me for the presentation and then added, "But there really is no need to be so defensive about this topic. We would not have come to your workshop if we weren't open to hear and learn from you." I do not mean to compare my journey to any one else's, nor to pretend mine has been fraught with the injustice of so many others, but for me that moment gave an insight that has been helpful in my repertoire of mindsets. A proactive voice is more readily heard than a reactive one.

A voice that speaks softly—as one who comes ready to build a bridge towards shared understanding—and carries great weight through the veracity of their information, morality of their message, and credibility of their personal story, has great influence.

LONGEVITY

ANOTHER ATTRIBUTE OF EFFECTIVE VOICES is their longevity. There will be many early spur-of-the-moment opportunities to speak and act about things that are just the right thing to say or do. However, when it comes to developing our voice in bridge building ways, we can anticipate that we are going to be in this for a while. Two stories may help explain this. You may have seen the fascinating pictures of bridges in Northeastern India that are not built but grown. In this humid area, crisscrossed by streams and rivers, the War-Khasis, a tribe in Meghalaya learned to train the strong root systems of a local rubber tree to grow out across the river. Eventually the roots connect to those of a tree growing on the other side. Some of these bridges are over one hundred feet long, can hold up to fifty people at a time, and have been used daily for over five hundred years. They are called Living Bridges. The responsibility for caring for and guiding the roots is often given to one family and passed down from one generation to another. Bridge Building Leaders understand that the bridges they are seeking to build may take years of careful nurture if they are to be living bridges.

LONGEVITY
(CONT'D)

The second story is quite different. I met Alice when attending some NGO meetings parallel to the UN Commission on the Status of Women in Manhattan. She was delightful. Standing shoulder high to the rest of us, with grey hair and kind eyes she was taking responsibility for ensuring we all knew where to meet for dinner. Alice was soft spoken, compassionate, inclusive and humorous—the perfect grandmother figure. Later that day, in a large group meeting I heard someone stand to address what someone in the panel had just said. Turning to see who it was I was floored to see my new friend Alice. The tiny grandmother transformed into a lioness as her voice spoke out with great clarity and authority about something she obviously knew a lot more about than the young whippersnapper on the stage. I had to bite my lip to keep from laughing with joy. When Alice stood, eighty years of advocacy and action rose with her. When she spoke it was with the voice of one who had the right to speak and had something important to say. I don't know at what point Alice found her voice, but on that day I trembled knowing I had just heard something profound and majestic. I had heard a trained, seasoned, powerful voice come out of a tiny but mighty person. Not surprisingly the whole room listened. Indeed there was a palpable energy that bounced back and forth across the room for a full, silent moment after she sat down. A lioness had just roared. And we all knew it.

I would later learn that the Reverend Canon Dr. Alice Medcolf graduated top of her class in applied Mathematics in 1958 but later dedicated herself to "the pursuit of justice in matters of gender, sexuality, and ethnicity."[171]

Alice was following in the footsteps of many influential grandmothers. Susan Anthony was a prominent civil rights leader who campaigned against slavery and for the promotion of women's and worker's rights. She traveled the United States and Europe, giving seventy-five to a hundred speeches per year, for forty-five years. Susan died fourteen years, five months and five days before the 19th Amendment was passed, giving women the right to vote. But she never gave up. In fact one of her most famous sayings was: "The older I get, the greater power I seem to have to help the world; I am like a snowball—the further I am rolled, the more I gain." Longevity builds momentum.

FOR MANY WOMEN, the journey to finding our voice is a living thing. It is a lengthy thing. It is a sacred thing. We see this in the keening of women down through the ages. In our laments and in our storytelling. In our protests and, for some, in our prayers. Standing alone and standing together. It grows from the burning in our bellies and our belief in a better future. Our voice is a powerful, purposeful, transformational tool. Bridge Building Leaders are wise to steward its development in themselves and others with great care.

A LIVING JOURNEY

ALSO, FOR MANY WOMEN, the journey to voice is closely linked to their vocational journey. Indeed, the words voice and vocation come from strongly related root Latin roots. Studies indicate that women, when starting out in their vocation, hold back because they do not feel they have anything important to say, or believe that, since they are in a junior position, it is not their place to insist that their viewpoint be heard. However, many senior leaders told of a breakthrough moment in which either holding back led to a failure, or they were given the floor by a senior person and made a contribution that led to a success. From then on, they made a conscious decision to make their voice heard—and to insist that others they lead speak up as well.[172]

VOCATION

PERSONAL REFLECTION – Consider that the words vocation and voice come from the same Latin root, *vocare*, which means "calling"—what we are uniquely born to do. How does this cause you to think differently about voice? What about your vocation?

COMMUNITY
AFFIRMATION

FOR MANY WOMEN, VOICE IS AFFIRMED IN COMMUNITY. This is often through a complex and individualized pathway involving their own courage and determination as well as the positive feedback and opportunities offered by those whom they perceive as gatekeepers. These gatekeepers, as we mentioned earlier, begin with parents, teachers, and peers in a girl's early years. They continue through cultural norms expressed in the media, workplace, family, and broader community.

REFLECT – How has your community affirmed your voice?

Ko taku reo taku ohooho, ko taku reo taku māpihi mauria.
My language is my awakening,
my language is the window to my soul.
Māori Proverb

REFLECT – How has your voice caused an awakening within you or others?

Eleanor Roosevelt was the mother of five children, wife, and a political aide to American president F.D. Roosevelt. She campaigned for humanitarian causes, human rights, women's rights, racial equality, social change, and stable politics her entire life. She was the first First Lady to hold Press conferences in the White House, was a voracious writer, and helped to draft the 1948 UN Declaration of Human Rights. After her husband's death in 1945, Eleanor continued to be an internationally prominent author, speaker, politician, and activist.

One of my favorites of her many quotable quotes is: *"Great minds discuss ideas; Average minds discuss events; Small minds discuss people."* Continuing in her footsteps we will consider how important it is to use our voice well.

Sometimes we assume that voice is about assertiveness, about getting our point across. Bridge Building Leaders understand voice differently.

My favorite description is "threading instinct and experience into the fulcrum of sharp, clear expression. Born at the intersection of tentativity [sic] and certainty, it requires both vulnerability and presence…leaders need to find their own voices… to have voice is to be fully present, to feel counted in, and counted on, to have something to say, and to be heard."[173]

REFLECTION – How do you respond to this definition? What does it suggest to you about your voice?

CHILDREN'S FIRE

THE FOLLOWING STORY ILLUSTRATES TRUE VOICE AT WORK. In one Native American Community in the US it is said that the elders made important decisions through a careful process that ended at a Children's Fire.[174] Sitting around this fire, if it could not be proven that a decision would positively influence children seven generations out, the whole discussion would be reopened. This is what we mean by leaders who have found their voice. True voice can never be for oneself alone. True voice speaks for the yet unborn, the ones whose destiny we, often unknowingly, hold in our hand.

SINCERITY AND *KINTSUKUROI*

TRUE VOICE GROWS OUT OF OUR PERSONALITY AND PASSION. It grows out of our convictions and experience. It grows out of character. It speaks to our integrity—our wholeness and sincerity. Our grandparents grew up knowing that when they signed a letter "sincerely yours" it had meaning. However, we have lost both the art of letter writing and the understanding of what sincerity truly means. In Roman times, disreputable potters were know to fill cracks in their pots with wax before glazing them such that unsuspecting purchasers would only discover the flaw when the pot was heated. More reputable potters began to hang signs claiming their pots were *sincerus*—meaning "without wax." To end a letter with "sincerely" was therefore to sign one's name to the veracity of all that was written above. Imagine taking the time to reflect on every document, conversation and proposal so as to be able to with integrity attach our signature, and our reputation to it. Bridge Building Leaders understand that credibility is not dependent on perfection but it is dependent on sincerity.

Perhaps even more astounding is the Japanese art of *kintsukuroi*. In this tradition, breakage and repair were considered part of a piece's rich history, not a reason to be discarded, or a fact to be hidden. Pots with cracks were understood to have endured great heat and pressure and were therefore treated with great care. The cracks were filled with gold and lacquer, such that the pot was even more beautiful and strong after. The cracks were celebrated and enhanced. The journey of the pot—both through hard knocks and gentle care—was honored. Our voice grows out of the solid, noble, whole, and compassionate parts of our lives. However, it also includes the brokenness, the cracks, the wax, the drama, and the trauma. Bridge Building Leaders know how to tell the whole story, to use appropriate vulnerability as well as stories of victory and perseverance. Bridges built on anything less are shaky at best. As Dr. Brené Brown suggests, *"Have the courage to be imperfect... Let go of who you think you should be, in order to be who you are. Fully embrace vulnerability, because what makes you vulnerable also makes you beautiful."*

PERSONAL EXERCISE – Draw a simple pottery shape considering carefully what shape it should be—an open bowl, a tapered vase, a cup or chalice? Add words, images or lines to present any known cracks and reflect on how you have sought to hide these, and/or allowed them to become places of greater strength and beauty. In what ways does this exercise cause you to look at your voice differently?

LIFE-GIVING VOICE

BRIDGE BUILDING LEADERS RISK THE DANGER of sincerely and with the best of intentions actually making things worse rather than better. While we do not need to be perfect, we do need to use our voice with care and in a spirit of learning. One tool that is helpful in thinking about this is the Life Giving Voice Chart. The four quadrants represent four foci. It is only as these overlap that a sustainable Life Giving Voice is found.

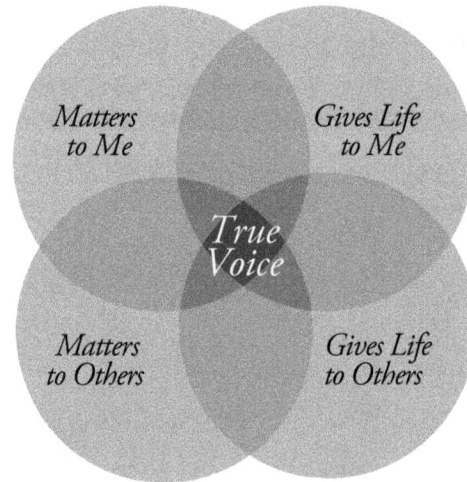

Figure 5. True, Life-Giving Voice.

THE MATTERS TO ME VOICE may be directive and assertive. It advocates well but may not listen well. There are times this voice is needed but its excessive use may indicate advocacy that is purely self-serving.

THE GIVES LIFE TO ME VOICE is compassionate to self and understands her own needs and preferences. While our true Voice will not always be so kind to self we will burn out if we neglect this part of our message for too long.

THE MATTERS TO OTHERS VOICE listens well but does not advocate well. It tends to minimize its own perspective and may be passive or avoidant. Like any of the Voices it has a powerful place when used in healthy ways but can quickly undermine one's confidence and impact if misused.

THE GIVES LIFE TO OTHERS VOICE is compassionate to others and seeks to understand others' needs and preferences.

The "sweet spot" of this diagram is found where the four Voices overlap. When we are advocating and seeking input, aware of our own and other's needs and preferences, seeking a creative, wise and sustainable "third way." Russian philosopher, Mikhail Bakhtin expresses this potential in a theory of dialogue that stressed the power of genuine conversation to increase understanding of multiple perspectives and create a myriad of possibilities.[175] This is voice at its best. This is the kind of voice needed by Bridge Building Leaders.

While voice transcends speaking, it does include it. Interestingly, "studies repeatedly, but not always consistently, find that it is men who do the talking and women who do the listening... That the actual behavior of the two sexes can be so discrepant from the stereotype is puzzling."[176]

DISCUSS – has this been your experience? Do the women on your team speak up as much as the men do? Why or why not?

The way we think about language and voice is important. Some Australian Aboriginal and Torres Strait Islander peoples going on *walk about* believe that the words they chant "sing their world into existence."[177] This is deeply profound when we pause to think of it.

REFLECT – In what ways do your words become reality?

LIFE GIVING VOICE
(CONT'D)

You may have heard the research that 38% of communication is tone of voice, 55% from body language and only 7% from words. This commonly taught but actually incomplete maxim comes from a small study[178] done for a particular purpose in 1960. Subjects listened to tape recorded words with or without pictures with facial expressions to see if they could accurately determine the motive of the speaker when saying words. The reality is that all are important and overlapping in terms of their impact on effectiveness. Bridge Building Leaders consider all parts equally and they take into consideration the multiple hidden lens we all wear. Or, as Richard Rohr wisely says, *"Most people do not see things as they are; rather, they see things as they are."*

TRUTH AND STORYTELLING

BRIDGES ARE BUILT CONVERSATION BY CONVERSATION. Story by story. Symbol by symbol. Breakthrough insight by breakthrough insight. Layer upon layer they influence our thinking and therefore our behaviour. BRAVE Leaders wisely leverage the power of conversation, setting, and story for transformational change.

In olden days knowledge, healing and art were considered inseparable. The architecture of ancient Greek amphitheatres were so well constructed for human audiences that the acoustics were phenomenal. Even the steps in the aisles leading down to the stage were hewn at specific distances so as to cause your steps to measure out the rhythm of the hexameter (a metrical line of verse). The great stories of what it meant to be human were told such that souls could be cleansed in a great catharsis, mysteries of life explored, and insight and transformation gained.[179] This is the power of word—and especially of *Wordeeds*.

DISCUSS – In what ways does architecture intersect with story telling? How does design influence your work space?

The Anishinaubaeg People of Canada have long held a high view of storytelling, truth and language. The highest compliment or tribute to pay a speaker was to say of him or her, *w'daeb-wae,* meaning he/she had cast their knowledge as far and wide as they have perceived it and as accurately as they can describe it. It is an affirmation of credibility, not infallibility as it was understood that no human held absolute truth. This credibility could easily be lost through careless speech. Once the bond of trust was broken, confidence in the speaker was lost and they no longer had influence with the audience. The worst epithet was to say "w'geewi-animoh" meaning one who talks in circles as a dog barks in all directions in uncertainty as to the source of some unknown disturbance.[180] Hence language, integrity and even identity were closely linked.

For the Mohawk people of Canada lying was considered such a serious "crime" that a "conviction" followed you for life and three such convictions led to banishment from the community![181]

Many cultures use parable and story telling to evoke deep thinking which enables us to not only describe but also transform our situations; therefore, storytelling is one of the greatest tools in a bridge builders tool-kit.

DISCUSS – how myths and stories can bring a different kind of truth.

"The shortest distance between truth and a human being is story."
Anthony De Mello

Peruvian author and Literature Nobel Prize winner, Mario Vargas Llosa's *The Storyteller* focuses attention on stories as the essence of a culture. He says effective Storytellers must penetrate the heart of a culture and provocatively claims that stories are something that the very existence of a people may depend on.

DISCUSS – the role of storytelling in the development of cultures where people can thrive.

TRUTH AND STORYTELLING
(CONT'D)

After a lifetime of "work, research and play" with storytelling and the social arts, author and founder of a Nordic Healing Story Training, Inger Lise Oelrich wrote, "The ongoing eruptions of war and armed conflict in the world are direct expressions of the breakdown of speech and dialogue in a community... The power of the living word between people is replaced by the sword of destruction."[182] Later in her book, Inger poetically explains that storytelling strengthens the Knight so she or he can confront and kill the dragon (internal or external)... and reminds us that our story fits into the context of a meta-story and therefore matters deeply.[183]

Storytelling can also help the Knight to choose more wisely their enemy. In one classic Celtic story, two warriors, each representing their country, face each other on the battlefield. Equally skilled and strong they fight the whole daylong. At night, falling to their knees from exhaustion they lay back and look at the stars, panting to catch their breath. After a time one begins to talk wondering how his sons at home are doing. The other listens then describes his wise wife and brilliant daughters. Looking out over the setting sun they are touched by the vibrant reds and oranges, later by the shooting stars, and finally by the rising sun. Each vista leads to story telling; each story to deeper insight. When at last day rises they stand, remove their armour and part as friends.[184] Propaganda leads to war, thoughtful story telling can lead to peace. This is why some peacekeeping initiatives are experimenting with mythological, parable and real-life storytelling.

REFLECT – How are the stories you are listening to and telling impacting the world around you?

TRADITIONALLY, MANY FACTORS HAVE IMPACTED women leaders' sense of not having a voice. Research shows that girls and women have more difficulty than men in asserting their authority or considering themselves as authorities;[185] in expressing themselves in public so that others will listen;[186] in gaining respect of others for their minds and their ideas;[187] and in fully utilizing their capabilities and training in the world of work.[188] "In everyday and professional life, as well as in the classroom, women often feel unheard even when they believe they have something important to say."[189]

This is complicated further by many women's beliefs that if they develop their powers it will be at the expense of others, if they excel others may be penalized, and that they should be selfless.[190] As research on girl's development demonstrated,[191] girls will often sacrifice their own voice for the sake of "saving" relationships with their friends.[192] Many girls choose not to become leaders because they fear making decisions, having ideas that are different from their friends, or appearing too achievement-oriented... girls feel pressured to choose between relationships and leadership.[193]

Barsch and Cranston, reiterating the well-known phenomena that many women are reluctant to speak up also suggest that "maybe that reluctance to speak masks deeper fears, such as the fear of being 'found out', the fear of being ridiculed, or the fear of being found unworthy... Our interviews suggest that fear drives many women to set an unrealistically high bar that would stop anyone... others confuse respect with remaining silent."[194] One result of this is seen in a study which compared the average woman's self-perception of their boldness upon entering a room or conversation against other people's perception of the same event. It showed that most women gauge their presence as more forcefu than others do.[195] Socialized to be quiet and then penalized for it, it is no wonder that many women have not yet found their voice.

WOMEN AND VOICE

REFLECT – Does fear play a role in your willingness to speak up? If so, how has this affected or limited you? If not, what inner belief has protected you from this?

As one woman wrote: "On every leadership team I've joined over the years, I have always felt like the experiment, the exception, the only one who sometimes wore a skirt and who didn't belong in the boy's club."[196] She is describing what is sometimes called the freight of being iconic. It is not uncommon. "Many individuals who find themselves in the minority experience the weight of representing their entire race or gender well."[197] I have sometimes felt this pressure as the only woman in the room. Perhaps you have as well. The question becomes what we do with this additional sense of responsibility. Many years ago a smart woman I knew gave one of the wisest pieces of advice I have yet heard about speaking in public. She challenged us to use every opportunity wisely. To come prepared, to speak well, and to assume our opinion mattered. I did not realize how important her advice was until overhearing a senior leader comment on the rambling way a young intern gave an announcement at an all staff meeting. He had been debating inviting her to participate as part of a special project team, but seeing how unprepared she was for this announcement, decided on the spot to ask someone else. Use your voice wisely.

THIS IS IMPORTANT FOR BRIDGE BUILDING LEADERS TO LEARN. However, it is equally important to be sure we do not fall into the same trap of judging someone's leadership ability from the way they make one announcement. One time I was chatting with a teacher from a youth leadership development initiative asking how the yearlong program was going. I asked him to point out some of the students who stood out. He mentioned several of the young men in the program. I asked which young women were demonstrating strong leadership ability and he—with some obvious embarrassment—noted that none did. Intrigued, I asked what attributes they were lacking that would cause him to say this. He explained that during group discussions the guys were much more likely to speak up more quickly and to hold their ground in debates. I asked if he knew that many women express respect by listening before speaking and see conversation as an opportunity to learn not just get their point across. The look on his face said it all. Hopefully more young women were given deeper consideration after that conversation.

For, of course, it is easy to be told to "speak up and speak well" and another thing to do it. The work of Cornell Academy of Management professor, James R. Detert, greatly contributes to our understanding of women's perceived sense of voiceless-ness. According to his and others' work[198] a significant portion of someone's sense of voice is predetermined by previous experiences, often at an early age. Here we see one more reason for early and intentional intervention in girls' and womens' lives. The initiatives being taken by schools, camps and girls' organizations can be hugely beneficial. They help young women develop a strong sense of self and a willingness to articulate their views and make decisions that impact themselves and others.

BRADY WILSON, CORPORATE TRAINER AND AUTHOR of *Juice: Release Your Company's Intelligent Energy Through Powerful Conversation,* writes, "*More problems are caused by missing conversations than by failed conversations.*"

DISCUSS – Do you agree? What conversations have you been avoiding out of fear they might cause problems? Is there a different way of thinking about the conversation you need to have?

We can envision a continuum of healthy and unhealthy approaches to potentially challenging conversations:

Passive _____ Assertive _____ Aggressive

DISCUSS – verbal and nonverbal examples of these three approaches and their impact on the whole group and process.

For the sake of our purpose here we can envision passive participants as essentially saying, "I don't want to contribute an opinion or make a decision" or more simply, "You win." Passive participants may be more difficult to read as they may be truly engaged and listening or they may be afraid to give an opinion. They may also be passive aggressive—more likely to talk after the meeting than during the meeting, not willing to contribute because they are angry or quietly sabotaging the process.

For this model we envision aggressive participants as those saying, "I have an opinion and will out talk (or shout) you if I need to" or, more simply "I win." Aggressive participants may be noisy and dominating the conversation or quietly manipulative, some people use silence for power believing information is power and therefore they will not share it. Some people, by just being in the room, shut down conversation.

Assertive participants according to this model are essentially saying, "I truly want to learn and therefore want to fully hear you." And, "I have some thoughts that I think will add to this conversation." This approach respects both self and others perspectives. This is important because "[t]he instant people perceive disrespect in a conversation, the interaction is no longer about the original purpose—it is now about defending dignity."[199]

The key is to approach conversations with a Bridge Building mindset as well as a strategy and tool belt of options… and since we often don't know in advance that a conversation will turn critical we need to be prepared for what may otherwise blindside us.

Peter Senge's work on voice in dialogue is both insightful and gender friendly. Noting the similarity between the words concussion, percussion, and discussion, he imagines a discussion as two or more people standing on opposite sides of a river, shouting at the same time in the foolish hope of being not only heard, but also understood. No wonder so many of us, men and women alike, lack interest in this model.

DIALOGUE
(CONT'D)

Dialogue, he suggests, offers a completely different way of engaging. In true dialogue, two or more people approach each other from opposite sides of a river as before. However, this time they step into the river and begin to move downstream together, trusting that they will come to a new place as a result of their speaking and listening. For this model to work, two things are necessary. Firstly, there must be respect and maturity. Secondly, each participant must practice what he calls "Advocacy and Inquiry." Advocacy means preparing, formulating, and being willing to deliver an opinion. Inquiry means asking what the other thinks and truly listening to the response. We sometimes think of this as a two-handed conversation. In one hand I bring a carefully developed opinion that matters deeply to me. My other hand is empty and open—ready to receive something that might add to, detract from, or very often provide a third way of thinking about the issue.

Dialogue—from the Greek *dia logos*—literally means *the word between*. In storytelling there is the storyteller, the audience, and the story. However, wise storytellers understand there is another variable: the space between these three elements. This space both separates and connects. It is also the most powerful of the characters in the storytelling scene. It is where the magic happens. Similarly, in dialogue, the space between is considered important, or almost sacred. This is the place of possibility, the place where breakthrough is possible, and where transformation can occur.

DISCUSS – Where have you experienced true dialogue recently? What did it create space for?

True dialogue depends on intentional listening. University professor and corporate consultant, Gervaise R. Bushe, describes the filters that interfere with our ability to listen as part of our mental map systems. He suggests that when it comes to listening:

1. Many of us have listening maps, things we expect to hear when interacting with others and listen mainly for these items.
2. We listen for what is on our maps and tend not to hear what isn't.
3. We often enter a conversation with a map of where we want the conversation to go and how we want others to respond.[200]

REFLECT – What listening traps are you most likely to fall into?

The Chinese character for listen is pronounced, "ting" and is made up of various parts representing the heart, the mind, the ears and the eyes. Two additional parts represent the speaker and the king. Traditionally, royalty sat with arms crossed (illustrated in the bottom left of the character), listening to ensure they had all the information before making a decision. This suggests the importance of bringing the whole person to listening but it also speaks to the additional importance for leaders. To listen like this is to listen like a Bridge Building Leader. It involves bringing one's whole self to the process and suspending assumptions until all the information is gathered.

*A voice is a human gift; it should be cherished and used to utter as fully
human speech as possible.
Powerlessness and silence go together.*
Margaret Atwood

VOICE AND POWER

JAMES DETERT, WHOSE WORK WE MENTIONED EARLIER, explores the link between voice and power. He demonstrates that specific power equalizing behaviours such as sitting side-by-side instead of across a desk and even the choice of locations—such as meeting in their office rather than yours—can encourage people to speak up more readily.[201] These variables help explain why subordinates become tongue-tied when talking to their superiors and many women, finally given the floor, struggle to find their voice.[202]

Indeed, we cannot think about leadership, social justice, or voice without considering the issue of power. *Fortune* magazine once asked the question, "Power: Do Women Really Want It?" Many of the women leaders quoted in the article, "expressed discomfort with the traditional demands of power and the inclination for seizing it for its own sake."[203] While women often see power as a negative thing, associated with its abuse, its original French root means simply, "to be able." It is only as we reframe power as something helpful, authentic, and life-giving that it can be fully embraced. Many women define power as energy and strength, rather than domination and control; or as something to be taught and shared, seen in relational terms with attributes such as cooperation and interdependence, rather than a model of competitiveness and dominance. Therefore, women's ways of leading tend to be more educational in nature, sharing information and expertise so that others can become effective as organizational participants and leaders as well.[204]

No wonder, "[w]omen do not usually feel comfortable with the power structures in their organizations. Hierarchy itself, and its implicit positioning of people into one-up, one-down positions, is actually far from women's search for establishing series of relationships between equals."[205]

The use and abuse of power has been an area of study for me for over twenty years. Few things are more pervasive and less openly discussed. From the interaction you may have had with a 2-year-old this morning about brushing their teeth, to the kids in the playground choosing who gets to be king of the castle, to a teenager out past curfew, to the discussion over who gets the remote or the best office, to the board debate about budget issues for next year… Issues of power are everywhere you look.

DISCUSS – What has been your experience of your own and others' view of power? How comfortable are you with the concept of personal power? What experiences and messages have helped to craft your view of power and the kind of power you wish to exert?

One of the most influential political leaders of the eighteenth century was Catherine the Great. She played an important role in improving the lot of the Russian serfs and placed great emphasis on the arts, literature, and education. Under her leadership Russia became one of the dominant countries in Europe. During her reign the Russian Empire expanded, improved its administration, and modernized. In fact, Catherine's rule revitalized Russia. Catherine was no stranger to power and intrigue. She ruled after a conspiracy deposed her husband, Peter III. However, Catherine understood power differently from her peers. She once said: *"Power without a nation's confidence is nothing."*

DISCUSS – the above quote. Do you agree? If so how would this principle apply in your context?

VOICE AND POWER
(CONT'D)

Our view of power significantly effects our voice and confidence level. In a fascinating study of indirect aggression among women, Heim and Murphy discovered a triangle of power, relationships, and self-esteem, saying, "There is a complex relationship between these elements—how much we have of one can affect how much we have of another." However, the correlations are not necessarily what we would expect. Women often avoid symbols of power such as educational degrees, titles, a striking figure, or outward confidence, believing they "inadvertently create obstacles when you are dealing with other women."[206] These naunced forces create many challenges.

REFLECT – Have you observed this phenomenon? What were the outcomes?

TRAIN-WRECK MOMENTUM
MODEL

THIS IS COMPLICATED FURTHER by the following common scenerio. Imagine that you are walking down the street and someone you know passes by on the other side without waving or saying "hi." Often, in these, or many other situations, our brain quickly jumps to conclusions —often, negative conclusions—about why this happened. "She hates me or she is ignoring me because of what happened last Tuesday, I can't believe she is holding a grudge about something so minor…" When in fact it may be that she just did not see us. Unfortunately once our brain has drawn a conclusion we see everything through that lens. Now we start to feel some emotion (frustration, anger, disappointment, hurt). These emotions and lenses link quickly to other similar experiences we have had in the past, views we have of ourselves, fears, sense of inadequacy, harsh words others have said when we were a kid etc. All of this "luggage," like cars on a freight train that is difficult to stop or slow down, come rushing up with us when we see that person the next time.

Not knowing why we just reacted the way we did, the other person now comes charging into our next meeting with their own freight train full of information, misinformation, feelings, past experiences, fears etc.

If this continues unchecked we will have a communication train wreck —with no just cause. Not all people "explode" in these kinds of situations. Some people "clam up"—making it difficult to know what they are thinking or what the freight they are bringing is.

Imagine how much more this happens for more serious misunderstandings, differences of opinion, or observed behaviours. Imagine how widespread trauma and historical abuses of whole people groups build massive trains with powerful momentum.

Discuss – How we can positively channel the energy of the train behind each of us? This can be profoundly difficult, especially in complex conversations and with hurtful histories. We begin to see how complex many of the interpersonal situations we face are and how deeply we need skilled and wise Bridge Building Leaders.

At a conference in Whitehorse, Canada about Native justice, Charlie Fisher, an Elder from Northern Ontario and Canada's first fulltime Native Justice of the Peace, explained how conflict was addressed in earlier times in Whitedog Falls. If, for example, a young person committed a crime against a shopkeeper the two would each be joined by a Representing Elder and sit in a circle to dialogue. They did not discuss the crime, their feelings, the impact, restitution or anything to do with the event. Rather, they sat on the floor as equals. The duty of the Representing Elders was not to speak for the two parties but rather to speak to them privately on the side until they were convinced that "the person's spirit had been cleansed and made whole again." Once this had occurred a ceremonial peace pipe was passed symbolizing that each had been "restored to the community and to him or herself."[207]

Discuss – In what way does this story cause you to think differently?

VOICE AND RELATIONSHIPS

AUTHENTIC RESTORATION IS AN IMPORTANT INSIGHT WHEN WE RECALL the importance of rich relationships to many women. As one author describes it, "[w]hen we feel accepted and validated by others, we reconnect to our inner selves and to the world around us… For women leaders, the affirmation and support of a larger community are still uncommon… Women leaders… are constantly reminded—subtly and not so subtly—that we are not truly welcome as we attempt to impart perspective or advocate a point of view. This type of repeated rejection has a profound effect. We doubt our own idea, intuition, and knowledge. We lose our self-esteem, confidence and desire to contribute."[208] How then are we to reconcile these opposing forces?

By putting ourselves down. It turns out that talking about personal problems is a way for a woman to willingly diminish her power in front of her peers and a common strategy to equalize perceived differences.[209] Not surprisingly, this further impacts our already faltering confidence. Heim and Murphy note that, "women not only diminish their self-esteem through negative self-talk; they also fail to compensate for it by building themselves up when they experience success. We usually attribute our accomplishments to factors outside ourselves."[210] If we have been tempted to act in this way perhaps this research helps us understand why. It also gives us the opportunity to reflect on whether or not we think this is a healthy way to act or what we would like to model to our daughters.

In this triangle of power, relationships, and self-esteem, the correlation between power and self-esteem is also of note. While, as one would expect, there is a correlation between women with higher self-esteem and higher achievement (in other words women with higher self-esteem are more likely to achieve), high achievement did not necessarily result in higher self-esteem.[211] This is the cause of many women's "imposter syndrome"—when her external power exceeds her self-esteem.[212] Isn't that interesting? Not only does higher achievement not increase our self-esteem, it may actually diminish it as we seek to minimize our success to fit in and as more angst arises about whether or not we have truly earned it.

DISCUSS – Have you observed any of the behaviours noted above? How would you like to process this?

Our stories about power—who has it and who doesn't—are woven into beliefs and mental models socialized by gender, ethnic group, culture, and family. They form a personal frame of reference affecting how we experience others, the world, and ourselves. The degree to which we consider ourselves power-full or power-less has broad and lasting implications.[213]

Ann Oakley explains some of the implications of women being seen as a minority group. "Members of minority groups tend to exhibit certain kinds of behavior; for example they will place a low value on their own abilities, prefer to avoid conflict, dislike one another… and appear helpless or overemotional… because the power relationships between dominants and subordinates identify self-importance, strength and rationality as human standards denied to 'subordinates.'"[214] Consider how this is amplified for women of color, differing ability, or any other minority group.

ONE OF THE MODELS I HAVE FOUND MOST HELPFUL in thinking about power is by Janet Hagberg. The model demonstrates the interaction between our inner and outer journeys as our influence expands through personal transformation. While described as stages, this imagery is not meant to be restrictive. Although we tend to have one stage where we are most at home, all the stages are within us and we may see glimpses of them throughout a given day.

I also like this model because it reminds us that our journey is toward wisdom and that the quest is worth the pain of getting there. In fact, this model suggests that the way we handle the adversity of our lives becomes a key determinant of the kind of person we become. Throughout the ages people have understood wisdom as more than a helpful attribute. It is a critical factor in leadership. Janet teaches that true leadership doesn't even begin until stage four and yet her research suggests many if not most leaders are functioning at stage three or lower levels. Scary. And not what is needed for Bridge Building leadership.

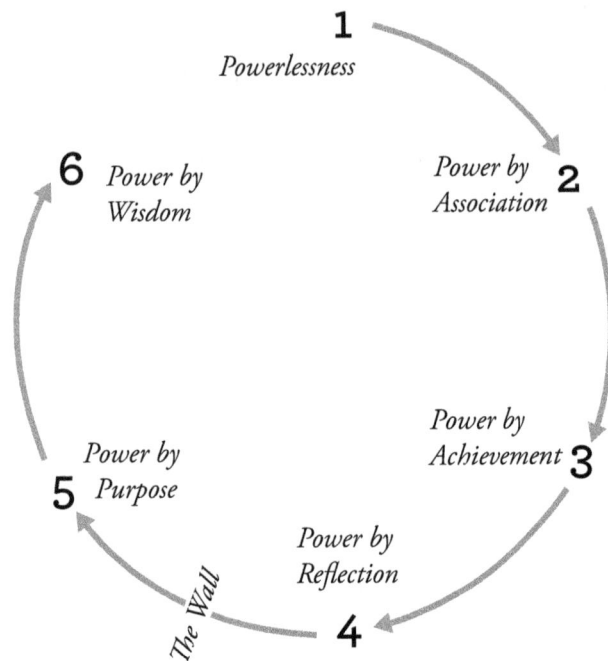

REAL POWER MODEL
Figure 6. Stages of Power
Reprinted with permission.

- The Stoics used the word *sophia* to describe wisdom—understood as knowledge of both the human and the Divine and critical to living a moral life.
- Ancient Hebrews personified Sophia as the wisdom of God—a woman in whom God delights. Hebrew kings were required to write out and read regularly the ancient texts that would enable them to lead with wisdom.
- The Qu'ran teaches that to whom wisdom is granted is indeed granted abundant good.
- The Eleventh Century Abbess, Hildegard of Bingen, described Sophia as "the encompassing energy of God whose one wing soars in heaven while the other sweeps the earth; quickening all she touches with life."
- The word "Philosophy" literally means friend of wisdom. In literature rulers of Utopia were expected to be philosopher kings.[215]

Wisdom is incredibly important for Bridge Building Leaders and a critical balancing factor for one's increasing power. Our journey towards it is enhanced by our ability to make sense of the experiences of our lives, lean into rather than run from the challenges we face, and reflect on what is truly important. Walking through the stages of the model together may help us to do this.

We are born into the world powerless to make decisions for ourselves. While many are able to move on from this stage as soon as they develop some independence, others—often due to illness, extreme poverty, disability, or abuse—cannot. Even those who have the resilience, resources, or role models needed to develop beyond this stage may find themselves back there. In fact, Hagberg suggests that every major change draws us temporarily back to this stage.

As noted earlier, many people have a love-hate relationship with power. Yet my experience is that unless we come to grips with what healthy personal power means, it will not only cause us to get stuck, but also create the kind of atmosphere where overreaction is likely. For example, "a girl will often passively accept repression for years without question. But once she becomes aware of a dissenting inner voice, the girl begins to wake up and dream of getting free… This new awareness is painful, but it also triggers other questions. If she is not what others want her to be, then who is she? What is her purpose in life? What does she want from life?"… she must overcome her own internal resistance to change.[216] The quest for self, the issue of voice, and our perspective of power are closely linked.

The metaphor of epic quest is perhaps apt here, for as well as knowing herself, a women must also reclaim those parts of herself that society devalues—this can be a more difficult and longer process than we think and internalized messages may have power over us long after we think we have rejected them.[217]

Real Power Model

Stage One: Powerlessness

"Women who don't take responsibility for their own lives
are often doomed to live out their lives like [the Mythical character]
… forever stuck in a cave they could walk out of anytime.
Recognizing one's own unconscious behavior, naiveté and complicity
is the key to finding one's power."[218]

It takes great courage to speak up against an authority figure (boss, partner, parent, religious leader). It feels so much safer to stay silent. *"But if one remains silent too long, one may choke to death on all those unsaid words."*[219]

REFLECT on the quotes above and note any areas where you have been silent or stuck for too long.

IN THIS STAGE OUR PERSONAL POWER COMES as a result of our association with someone or something. I speak as so-and-so's wife or I come in the name of the organization I represent. Many women get stuck at this stage, often because they dislike what they see in the next one. It is helpful to remember to,

Be like the bird that, pausing on her flight awhile on boughs too slight,
feels them give way beneath her, and yet sings, knowing that she hath wings.
Victor Hugo

PEOPLE IN STAGE THREE ARE EASILY IDENTIFIED. They look successful and act successfully. They are competent and confident. The symbols that suggest status will look different culturally, organizationally, and personally. They may be anything from a corner office to a grand master key, from a good education to a charismatic personality, from expensive clothes to a confidence that elicits trust from others. There is nothing wrong with these things. It is just that they do not necessarily enable one to lead wisely or be skilled at Bridge Building.

Janet's research suggests that women are less likely to be attracted to this stage with its trappings of Western power, prestige, and organizational politics. Meanwhile leadership—in the West at least—is most commonly associated with this stage, and many organizations seek stage three leaders because of their perceived competence and confidence. It is perhaps no wonder that many women prefer to stay in stage two or resist staying in roles or organizations that trap them in stage three when their inner world exists in a stage four or five reality.[220]

However, for those with eyes to see, stage three represents a maturing of women's egos, the outward part of our personality that interacts with the world. Handled wisely this stage does not make us egotistical but it can make us stronger. According to Janet, women may not relate as much to the successful, achieving part but it is important to allow our egos to mature so we could stand up for ourselves and others. Stage three is also the place where we learn both competence and confidence. This is why it is so critical

REAL POWER MODEL

STAGE TWO: POWER BY ASSOCIATION

REAL POWER MODEL

STAGE THREE: POWER BY ACHIEVEMENT, STATUS, AND SYMBOL

for us to both grow into and through this stage well and to create room for other women to do the same. I remember the day a senior leader called to ask for help with a female member of their team I had been working with. He described the situation, suggesting her response was another low confidence issue that he needed to help her navigate. Yet even as he spoke I realized the opposite was true. Her words and actions indicated she was no longer making decisions based on what would please him. She had found the strength to say no to some things that were not right for her, a very different stance than not accepting an assignment due to fear. This was new and would take some time for both of them to adjust to. However as he came to see that it was a very healthy part of her development as a person and a leader he was better able to help create the space she needed. Without this kind of environment, many people feel the need to move on if they find themselves too constrained by old expectations and opportunities.

THIS STAGE REPRESENTS THE BEGINNING of the deepening inner journey—often prompted by disillusionment. Stage four leaders can be identified by their growing humility. They also stand out due to the growing number of people who want to be more like them. Ironically, for the individual this is the season of confusion because a deep work has begun in their lives that undermines their previous confidence while simultaneously enabling them to be more authentic and influential.

Here we begin to realize that the Wisdom to know what matters and the courage to do it are accessible to us… in our personal story, in the traditions of our families, in the myths and heroines of our culture, and in the lives of our friends and associates. Discovering these resources is part of the journey.

Any journey takes courage and includes surprises, both good and bad. An inner journey is the same and often involves suffering and lament, loss and disappointment, disillusionment and even despair. We have discussed how the way we handle adversity becomes an important piece in the people we become… but so does reconciliation, acceptance, forgiveness of self and others, break through, renewed hope and vision, and passion and beauty.

Kimiko Okano Murakami was born in British Columbia, Canada in 1904. Intelligent and resourceful, she learned to pilot her parents' fishing boat at five years of age. She was also the family banker. When Japan attacked Pearl Harbor in World War II the family was rounded up and taken to a "filthy, crowded animal barn." Three months later the family was finally reunited but not set free. Their property was confiscated and sold. They were forced to move multiple times from one internment camp to another. Many years later when they returned to British Columbia they were unable to purchase back their land. Both in their 50's, she and her husband started over on fresh scrubland and rebuilt their lives, becoming involved again in the community that had once betrayed them. Kimiko's daughter, Mary, said "The word bitterness was never a part of mother or father's vocabulary. The word spoken most often was forgiveness."[221]

SMALL GROUP DISCUSSION – Looking back over your lifetime what is one story that stands out as a defining moment that gave you strength to pursue who you are and who you are becoming? Where did the strength come from?

STORIES ARE IMPORTANT. They not only describe reality, but as we have seen, they can change reality—enabling us to imagine a new reality for ourselves or others. Jody Bower suggests there are differences between the epic journeys written by men and the stories written by women about women. Reflecting on these differences may enable us to understand our own journey better.

POWER AND STORY

- Hero myths involve doing—a great act of heroism that solves the problems of the hero and his realm. They are about coming home.

- Heroine myths involve being and becoming—They are about leaving home and wandering. Her acts of heroism are often unseen or not believed and her bravery comes in her willingness to carve her own path and refusing to do or be what others are insisting she must.

"The hallmark of [the heroine] is that she refuses to be trapped, either by others or by her own resentments or fears."[222]

*Figure 7. Your Life, Your Legacy
Collection: "Living." Hand-Woven
Textile.*

LITERATURE AND LEGEND, written by
women, for women, has traditionally
featured the motifs of weaving and wings.
It is as if these motifs embody the women's
contribution as they weave the many parts
of their lives. We know that when women
are empowered, communities are stronger.
However, these woven nets represent safety
and inclusion, not restiction—illustrated by
the second image of wings.

The fabric opposite was created by textile
artist Candice Ball of Way Through the
Wilderness Handwovens and is a contemporary example of this tradition.

- The hero transforms himself and preserves or restores the community, often bringing them back gifts he found on the journey.

- The heroine transforms community by bringing forth gifts from within herself while preserving or restoring herself.[223]

REFLECT – In what ways are your journeys transforming the broader community?

REAL POWER MODEL

THE WALL

MOVING BETWEEN ANY OF THE STAGES REQUIRES A LETTING GO of something and an adopting of something new and unknown. Nowhere is this more evident than at the Wall we encounter between stages four and five. It is as if the rug has been pulled from under us and our ways of coping and strategies for success no longer seem to work. The Wall is different for everyone. It may involve a deep loss, shame, or disappointment yet it is more than this, for almost everyone experiences these kinds of things sometime in their life. It is the inner response, the inner journey (that only some are willing to take) that accompanies this outer experience that creates a Wall. Some people describe this season as the dark night of the soul. Certainly it is a time of deep uncertainty. As everyone's wall is different no one can go with us or show us the way. To get through it we will have to find and adopt very different ways of thinking and acting.

I remember the day that it felt like I "broke." My beloved father-in-law had died suddenly. My mother, with whom I shared a close but complex relationship (as many women do) died less than a month later—the day after we had left home on a much-needed sabbatical due to work related burn out. Our children were young and experiencing some challenges of their own. My brother's epilepsy had worsened such that only a strict regime of ever-changing medications and stress-reducing techniques enabled him to get through the day. He made the courageous decision to have experimental brain surgery—a lengthy, excruciatingly painful and difficult surgery and recovery time. The night before his surgery I lay down on the back porch of my brother's home to look at the stars and felt something "break" inside me. I did not know what it was and had no clue how long it would take and what painful times we would need to go through as part of the healing journey.

"*Every change on our lives requires us to spend some time in 'liminal space', the space between the old life and the new, the person we were and the person we are becoming*"[224]… nowhere is this more true than at the wall, in the unknown wilderness, the dark night of the soul.

"*Even the most difficult path is a path made by others first. Changing paths requires leaving the one you are already on and crossing uncharted territory that is both full of obstacles and dangers and without any guarantee that you will strike another clear path.*"[225]

PERSONAL REFLECTION – Where are you in liminal space? What paths are you forging and how difficult is the journey these days?

No wonder we often feel lost here. We must find strengths within and around ourselves we did not need to access before. These strengths and sources will be important to the next stage of our lives and that is why we must take our time accessing them now.

REAL POWER MODEL

STAGE FIVE: POWER BY
PURPOSE

PART OF MY HEALING CAME during a sabbatical trip to Scotland—the land of my grandparents. I could never have imagined how viscerally I would experience this homecoming. Stepping off the plane, and throughout the month we spent there, as well as during visits since, I felt strangely connected to the land. Sometimes we can find great strength in our heritage.

My mother, two grandmothers and great grandmother were all Scottish. Women in Ancient Celtic society enjoyed rights that Greek and Roman societies did not have. A woman could own property, get a divorce, be a priest, a judge, a doctor, a poet, fight in battle and even own her own fighting school. She also had the right to rule. Celtic Women maintained their name through the matrilineal line and I have long identified, with my female lineage, as a MacDonald. Even so, nothing prepared me for the moment when, on a simple day out in the Highlands, our Scottish Tour Guide, stopping at Glencoe, cued the stirring bagpipe music, and began to tell the story of the massacre that happened there. Back in the day, Scots, like many people groups, were sworn to an unwritten rule of hospitality. Even enemies were guaranteed safety, sleep, and food in one's home.

The story goes that one night the Campbells, the MacDonald's longtime foes, arrived at nightfall requesting a warm place to shelter. The MacDonalds—who had by this time in the story become *my people* in my head—invited in the weary travelers, fed them and gave them warm bedding. Then, in the middle of the night the Campbell's allegedly arose to slaughter every MacDonald man, woman, and child they could catch. Those who survived fled into the valley, their bare feet burning on the snow covered rocks. My people. Slaughtered in their beds. Betrayed, even as they extended hospitality. I responded viscerally as rage roared up from my belly. Though normally a fairly passive person, I might have strangled any poor person by the name of Campbell who might have innocently been standing there. Why did I respond thus? The beauty of the scene was a contributing factor, as was the effectiveness of the story telling. However it went beyond this. I had tapped into something deep and powerful. My story. We can go often into our personal and cultural story to find strength and bravery.

We will need these additional resources because stage five is the place where spirituality, humility, self-acceptance and wisdom are inherently more powerful than ego. Believing in and beginning to represent to others a vision bigger than themselves, people in stage five are followed because their inner power and purpose are so much greater than those around them.

While it may be difficult to track our female heritage, since women have been written out of many history books or included only as a footnote, if we dig we can often find sources of strength and inspiration.

Women in a focus group in Russia explained that Russian women are like the supports that hold up the building. "A woman will sacrifice herself rather than let the building fall," they say. This metaphor helps these women during difficult times to find personal strength and to tap into something bigger, older, and more powerful than themselves.

Studying women's history we discover few of them relied on institutionalized authority. It was their personal power, spiritual and ethical strength, networks and countercultural strategies they relied upon. In the 1990 Oka crisis in Quebec, Canada, when the tension between government soldiers and Mohawk warriors escalated, it was the women who came, unarmed, stood in the incredibly dangerous zone between them and said, "Enough." Waneek Horn-Miller said this action was not unexpected. "The woman's job is to ensure the safety of the community, and that is including making sure the men don't step too far."[226] The men on both sides backed down and further bloodshed was averted.

SMALL GROUP DISCUSSION – what stories, traditions or cultural norms from your ethnic or religious heritage do you draw strength from?

REAL POWER MODEL

STAGE SIX: POWER BY
WISDOM

STAGE SIX REPRESENTS THE PLACE OF WISDOM, deep spirituality, deep personal sacrifice and unique creativity we all carry within us and may aspire to if we are willing to do the hard work of homecoming. The Mother Theresas of the world who live with this as their home stage, have come to represent something much larger than themselves. Not perfect people, stage six people are profoundly aware of, but no longer troubled by, their deep flaws.

As we reach back into our cultural heritage and listen to the stories of our heroes and heroines, we often see women celebrated as wisdom carriers. As I share one of my favorite stories perhaps you will sense how long ago the BRAVE Woman Bridge Building leader story was embedded in me.

When I was growing up, my mother's best friend, whom we called Aunt Lilas, came to visit frequently. When she did, I slept in the basement or in my parents' room so she could have my bed. She had strong opinions about how children should behave so, when Auntie was in the house we spoke in hushed tones and kept our elbows off the table. There were many reasons why I should have feared or disliked my Aunt. However, I adored her. She was the first person to take me to a restaurant with white tablecloths. She introduced me to ballet and to literature. She gave me the most delightfully age inappropriate gifts. For example, she gave me an antique copy of Pauline Johnson's poetry when I was barely old enough to read. Little did she know that in doing so she introduced me to one of the heroines I have carried with me from childhood. I still have that leather bound volume, but from age and use its cover must be kept wrapped in tissue to prevent it from disintegrating even further. Imagine my delight then when I moved to Muskoka and discovered that Pauline used to canoe and camp just around the bay from our home; and that she wrote one of her best known poems about our local river.

Born to a Mohawk* Chief father and English Lady mother—in an era where, sadly, in Canada First Nations people were only invited to the back door of English homes—Pauline Johnson lived in a house her father built in the 1850's near Brantford, Ontario that had two front doors. European colonists would come by road to the one door, Haudenosaunee guests to the other. Growing up in a house that served as a bridge between the two communities profoundly influenced Pauline.

Pauline's father, George Henry Martin Johnson, as a Mohawk chief, was an important member of the Haudenosaunee community. The Haudenosaunee practiced the most complex and intentional form of leadership I have yet to come across. It involved strong ties between six neighboring nations—the Mohawk, Cayuga, Onondaga, Oneida, Seneca, and Tuscarora. Each Nation maintained its own autonomy and Chief, yet all were connected through Clans that ran horizontally between the Nations. This created a woven matrix of leadership that ensured balance and wisdom.

The story of how this style of government came about is a classic story of Bridge Building.

Haudenosaunee Elder, Oren Lyons, tells of the time before the confederation when the nations were at war between and within themselves. It was a time of fierce hatred. A Peacemaker[227] arrived in the Mohawk community and was instructed to stay in the lodge of a woman who welcomed anyone travelling that path. Her only rule was that weapons of war and discussions of war be left outside the door. Later when the Peacemaker gathered the leaders of the nations on the shores of Onedaga Lake, in the heart of the five nations, the Onedaga did not join them. After much discussion the Peacemaker planted a Great Tree whose roots going in four directions represented the Great Laws that would enable the people to live in peace. Envisioned as one inclusive and ever expanding longhouse (Haudenosaunee means "the people building a longhouse" and was as much a philosophical and religious construct as a method of architecture) the Five Nations (and later Six) were represented by a beaded wampum belt with a tree in the center, pathways going in both directions linking the two nations on either side and extending east and west to invite others in.

REAL POWER MODEL

STAGE SIX: POWER BY
WISDOM
(CONT'D)

PAULINE JOHNSON

* THE MOHAWK PEOPLE are
part of the larger nation
called Haudenosaunee.

REAL POWER MODEL

STAGE SIX: POWER BY
WISDOM
(CONT'D)

PAULINE JOHNSON
(CONT'D)

The Peacemaker said, "We must go and gather the Onedaga in." Tadadaho, their leader was a wicked and powerful man who was content with things the way they were. Spending time with the Peacemaker changed him but he was still unwilling to join. So the Peacemaker called for the woman, who shared his vision for change. When she arrived the leaders asked if she knew how to bring Tadadaho out of the swamp where he lived and into the confederacy. She taught them a powerful song. When the leaders sang the song in a united voice Tadadaho came out of the swamp and joined the discussion. He became the 50th leader to join the circle. To this day the 50th leader has additional responsibility and authority. Represented by a beaded circle with 49 equal length strands radiating out and one longer than the others the Tadadaho has the power not of veto or of tie breaking but of consensus. During the Albany congress of 1754 Benjamin Franklin expressed his frustration that a dozen English colonies could not create or sustain a similar union.

Chiefdom was established through the matrilineal line. George's mother was an important member of the Wolf Clan. She was devastated when George married outside their Nation—thereby disentitling his sons to be future Chiefs—and threatened to never speak to him again. Pauline's mother's family was so upset about the marriage that they never spoke to the family again. Fortunately for all, George's mother had a change of heart. Hearing a first grandchild had been born, she arrived on their doorstep with gifts.

Emily Pauline Johnson was born in 1861. The year Abraham Lincoln became President of the United States. She was the youngest of four children. Her Mohawk name was *Tekahionwake*—pronounced: *dageh-eeon-wageh*, which meant literally: "double-life" or "Two Lives." As both a Mohawk woman and an English Lady, she signed her name with both signatures representing the two worlds she straddled.

When Pauline's father died, as a result of gunshot wounds sustained while protecting Mohawk lands from illegal hunting and deforestation, her family could no longer afford to keep the house. Pauline decided to carry on her father's work by using her life and vocation—writing and speaking—as a bridge between the two communities. Pauline has been one of my heroes since I was perhaps five years old. She was a quintessential Bridge Building Leader.

When speaking in England, Pauline advocated for the important causes her Haudenosaunee community espoused, including protecting the environment (at a time when England was locked in Industrial madness), equality amongst people groups (at a time when this was anything but the case), and equality for women (at a time when Suffragettes were lobbying for votes for women but women in traditional Haudenosaunee societies were almost equal in power and respect to men).

As we might imagine, Pauline was not always well received. Booed off stages, criticized in the press and dismissed by many friends and even family members, she carried on, travelling across Canada and the United Kingdom to speak and write.

I mentioned earlier my delight when, moving to Muskoka, I discovered that one of my favorite of Pauline's poems, "Shadow River," was written about the stream two kilometers from our home. In this poem Pauline reflects on reflection. Canoeing the river, as I often have since, one cannot help but notice the mirror-like surface of the water and the incredible beauty reflected in it.

Pauline realized that the power and beauty of the land was much bigger than herself. Yet just dipping her paddle, something she must do to move forward, would ripple the water and thus muddy the reflection. In this poem we see her deep love for nature, her awareness of both her smallness and her influence, and her desire for peace, yet willingness to make waves if necessary. As a poet, lecturer, speaker, and advocate for the environment, for peace, and for equality of the sexes she truly was a woman before her time. From an early age I was fascinated by the power of her passion and only later understood how difficult it must have been for a single women at that time to find and use her voice so bravely.

REAL POWER MODEL

STAGE SIX: POWER BY WISDOM
(CONT'D)

On the topic of women of wisdom, wit, and voice, I have to include one of my favorite stories. Agnes Campbell Macphail (1890-1954) was the first woman to be elected to the Canadian House of Commons and one of the first two women elected to the Legislative Assembly of Ontario. She was always a strong voice for rural issues, penal reform, women in the criminal system (leading her to found the Elizabeth Fry Society), worker's rights, pensions for seniors, pacifism and global disarmament. She was also the first Canadian woman delegate to the League of Nations in Geneva, Switzerland. Check out her classic sass in this quote of hers: "I do not want to be the angel of any home: I want for myself what I want for other women, absolute equality. After that is secured, then men and women can take turns being angels." Zinger.

GROUP DISCUSSION – what heroes and heroines do you draw from as you move forward on your inner journey?

Stage six is the place of wisdom, depth, and selflessness. It is also the epitome of redemptive creativity. The role of this kind of creativity should not be minimized in our personal and shared journey. From 2013-2014 1,726 pairs of beautiful but unfinished moccasin tops, called vamps, travelled across Canada in honor of the 1,000 Canadian missing Indigenous women.

As Estes once said,
"a single creative act has the potential to feed a continent."

The unfinished moccasins represent the unfinished lives of the women whose time was cut short. When the call was given for contributions, three times the number requested were sent, featuring a wide range of materials and styles reflecting many Indigenous cultures. The vamps were arranged in a winding path on the floor and the exhibit was called "Walking with our Sisters."[228]

Women who have grown into this kind of stage six power, often as a result of deep hardship balanced by insight, use it neither passively nor aggressively. Knowing just the right moment and trusting in counter intuitive partners, practices and processes, they enable wisdom and love to transform what was once thought immovable.

EXERCISE – Reflect on how voice is an important attribute of BRAVE Bridge Building Leaders. Where are there opportunities for you to practice this even more powerfully?

REFLECT on how your understanding of power has changed, if at all, as a result of this chapter?

REFLECT on how your power and voice are linked.

Thus far we have discussed how Bridge Building Leaders who long to see transformation in their world must find the bravery and resilience born of hope. To this we added the skills and mindsets of advocacy and action and the power of cultivating our voice. In the next chapter we will explore how Bridge Building Leaders seek an ever-expanding perspective supported by an ever-growing skill set to fuel their expanding influence.

The Journey
by Mary Oliver

One day you finally knew what you had to do, and began,
though the voices around you kept shouting their bad advice – – –
though the whole house began to tremble
and you felt the old tug at your ankles.
'Mend my life!' each voice cried.
But you didn't stop. You knew what you had to do,
though the wind pried with its stiff fingers at the very foundations – – –
though their melancholy was terrible. It was already late
enough, and a wild night, and the road full of fallen branches and stones.
But little by little, as you left their voices behind,
the stars began to burn through the sheets of clouds,
and there was a new voice, which you slowly
recognized as your own, that kept you company
as you strode deeper and deeper into the world,
determined to do the only thing you could do –
– determined to save the only life you could save.

Expanded Perspective, Skill, and Influence

*"Everyone thinks of changing the world, but no one thinks
of changing [the]mself."*
Count Leo Tolstoy, Russian novelist (1828-1910)

IT IS AN OFT' QUOTED MAXIM that we must "be the change we long to see."
And it is true. If we are going to become the kind of BRAVE women and
Bridge Building Leaders our world so desperately needs we must anticipate
that the transformation begin in us.

As Abigail Adams—wife of John Adams, the second US
President, and mother of John Quincy Adams, the sixth—
once said, "Great necessities call forth great leaders." Great
leaders don't just happen, they develop in response to great
need.

> *Great leaders don't just
> happen, they develop in
> response to great need.*

BRAVE Bridge Building Leaders understand that for the change to begin
with them, they will need to look differently at both themselves and their
world. As blogger Marilyn Gardner writes, "building bridges means moving beyond my enclave of cultural [and I would add personal] comfort

to a place of cultural humility and willingness to learn." The work begins first in their mind. Consider the following, powerful example, "When the opposition line up against the New Zealand national rugby team—the All Blacks—they face the *haka*, the highly ritualized challenge thrown down by one group of warriors to another... Opposing teams face the *haka* in different ways. Some try to ignore it, others advance on it, most stand shoulder-to-shoulder to face it. Whatever their outward response, inwardly the opposition know that they are standing before more than a collection of fifteen individual players. They are facing a culture, an identity, an ethos, a belief system—and a collective passion and purpose beyond anything they have faced before. Often, by the time the *haka* reaches its crescendo, the opposition has already lost. For rugby, like business [or most leadership endeavors] and much of life, is played primarily in the mind."[229]

REFLECT – In what ways is your life and leadership being played out in your mind and how is that affecting the actual outcome?

Since the work begins in our minds, wise Bridge Building Leaders adopt a Growth Mindset.[230] People with Fixed Mindsets believe their opportunity to change and grow is limited. Leaders increasingly are learning the importance of Learning Agility—the ability to learn from life experience in such a way that our brains actually develop new pathways and patterns. We remember that Nelson Mandela and many of his counterparts experienced the same things but only he allowed these experiences to shape him into the kind of thinker and powerful Bridge Building Leader he became.

DISCUSS – Where have you become stagnant in your thinking? What experience, way of thinking, or relationship might enable you to break out of this?

SEVERAL YEARS AGO, WE VISITED A FRIEND IN THE COUNTRY. Cicadas and birds were singing and the sky was brilliantly blue as we entered a showroom. It was early in the morning, late in the summer. The showroom was only open during daylight hours since natural lighting was used to protect and display the fascinating pieces. Our eyes and ears accustomed as we stepped out of the brightness of the morning into the muted light of the studio and walked its length in silence. Raphael unlocked the massive carved door into his shop. Smelling fresh wood we stepped into the darkened room.

EXPANDED PERSPECTIVE

Raphael walked to the first window, unlatched an antique wrought iron hook and swung open the heavy, rustic wood shutters. Sunlight streamed into the room. Visible rays illuminated the dust stirred by our footsteps. I gasped involuntarily as shutter after shutter swung open in the same theatrical fashion. We stood awestruck by the beauty and simplicity of the room. There was something glorious about the vibrant reds, greens, and yellows of hand-tied brooms hanging from every wall. The only sound was the cracking of ice as Raphael poured homemade mint tea into a jug on the rough-cut table in the center of the room.

Few times in my life compare with the beauty or insight of that moment—and yet it was the simplest of events—a visit with a friend, the drinking of iced tea, the purchase of a broom. The name of his Studio: The Radiance of the Ordinary.

This story remains a powerful part of my personal journey because it reminds me of two things—the beauty, power, and perspective when light pours in, and that the simplest of things can sometimes have a profound impact. In this chapter we come full circle to consider again what it means to be a Bridge Building Leader. Many women hesitate to lead due to fear, competing values or the expectations of others. Leadership that is BRAVE enough to build a bridge, enables us to move beyond these obstacles and to reflect on the possibility… the radiance of the ordinary.

EXPANDED PERSPECTIVE
(CONT'D)

Thousands of books are published each year on leadership. Make it a practice to stay current but also consider that no leader has ever read all these books. Leadership is both a science and an art. While staying open to input, learn to trust also that what you have is enough. Use personal reflection to uncover just how much you know. Use personal stories to explain your style and convictions. Use personal relationships to build your team. We do not always need to seek the extraordinary—we sometimes can discover the radiance in the ordinary.

REFLECT – If someone could flip a switch and give you fresh perspective in some area what area would that be? Who do you know that is very different from you in their life journey, worldview, and behaviour that you could learn a lot from?

An expanded perspective includes, but is not limited to, our growing understanding of how different personalities communicate, make decisions, become stressed, and best contribute. It includes a growing awareness of cultural differences.[231] And it includes a growing sensitivity to the gender and generational distinctives that can make or break someone's ability to fully sense that they belong and contribute.

Returning to the model of environments where women leaders thrive— explored earlier—we could build this out such that each element becomes a continuum. Each expresses a range of choices to represent environments where all types of people could thrive. This kind of model is best understood as a series of competing values. The values at each end are neither right nor wrong ways of thinking or working. They are polarities: seeming opposites that are both true. Cultures where both ends of the spectrum are celebrated and maximized are rare yet possible. They require Bridge Building Leaders skilled at what is sometimes described as the dance of polarities—able to move back and forth along the line depending on the situation, keeping the team in the positive zone of each and able to utilize the strengths of those who adhere to each pole.

If we were to represent these intersecting poles visually they would look like this.

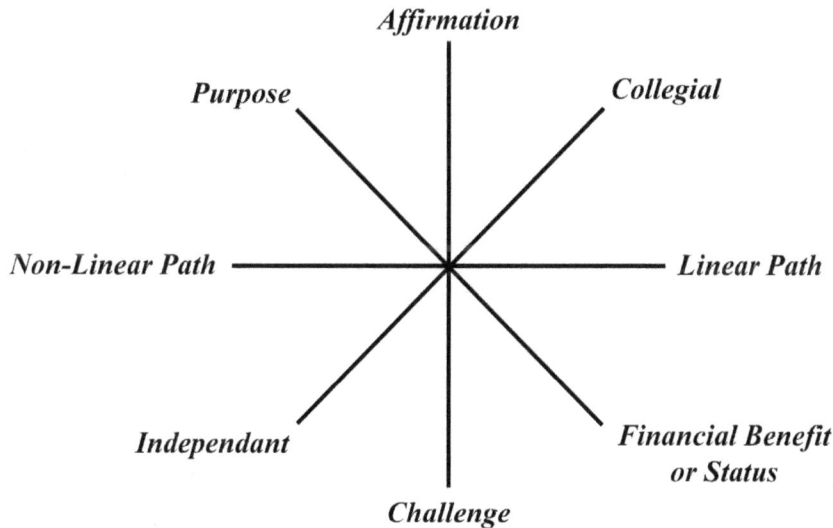

Figure 8. Balanced Teams and Workplaces Model

A STORY MAY HELP ILLUSTRATE. It may seem deceptively simple. Low-ropes courses are only a few feet off the ground, and lack most of the wow-factor of their high-ropes counterparts. So, it is no surprise when a team gathers beside the element known as the whale watch without much trepidation. Incase you haven't seen one, a low ropes whale watch station is essentially a large wooden raft supported by a central fulcrum that allows it to seesaw back and forth when not perfectly balanced. The goal is to get everyone onto the apparatus in such a way that it is perfectly balanced and unmoving for a period of one minute. To balance it, a team must do one of two things. Either everyone must stand in the very center—a simplistic solution most teams attempt initially, but soon discover becomes crowded and ineffective—or equal weight must be applied on each end. The latter is a more complicated and elegant solution. As you might expect it takes several tries, some choice words, and a few desperate lunges before the team learns the importance of moving slowly and collaboratively, each action counterbalanced by someone opposite them. Standing in the center of the whale watch, asking questions or making suggestions when necessary and adjusting her own weight back and forth ever so slightly to assist with the process, is a team leader. I never cease to be amazed at how one person's actions affect the whole. Frustration mounts as individuals grandstand or lose focus. Each member must both manage his or her own movements and work with someone at the other end of the seesaw to ensure success. It is more difficult than it looks and the more people involved the more challenging it becomes. It is a powerful metaphor for how Bridge Building Leaders empower teams to collectively balance the raft of diverse perspectives.

Teams and organizations sometimes use a competing values framework to plot their norms and decide when and where to flex and grow. This particular competing values model gives people who are serious about building environments where both men and women can thrive as leaders, a tool to stimulate dialogue and plot preferences. It is not intended as prescriptive so much as descriptive. In the Balanced Teams and Workplace Model, the non-linear path is counter-balanced by more traditional development paths. Purposeful work is balanced by financial and other motivators. Invitational and affirmational approaches are counterbalanced by opportunities for challenge and competitiveness. Collegial, relationship rich atmospheres are counterbalanced by opportunities for independence and autonomy. Skilled and brave Bridge Building Leaders are able to see the value of each polarity and help teams move with wisdom and flexibility back and forth along the continuums as needed. The tool can be used to help set expectations, create shared language and strengthen culture through a shared willingness to structure meetings, initiatives, and organizational cultures in thoughtful, inclusive ways.

THREE SKILLS CRITICAL TO DEVELOPING OUR PERSPECTIVE

1. NOTICING: The most basic of skills and yet one of the most difficult. Our worldview creates a set of lenses through which we, often unknowingly, view everything else.

EXPANDED PERSPECTIVE: THREE CRITICAL SKILLS

> *He rangi tā Matawhāiti,*
> *he rangi tā Matawhānui.*
> *The person with a narrow vision sees a narrow horizon,*
> *The person with a wide vision sees a wide horizon.*
> Māori Proverb

In the Leadership Studio, we explore the skill of noticing in several different learning experiences that you could adapt and use yourself or with your team. Just steps from our front door is a stream, spanned by a long suspension bridge. The bridge serves as the main entrance to the building and it is an experiential tool to teach leadership. Beside the stream, we have built a short trail and named it the Noticing Trail. The path is used in simple ways to cause us to slow down and pay attention to what is around and within us. The great irony is that people who have visited the site numerous times, and even people who live and work on other parts of the property, often mention that they have walked by and "never noticed it before." We walk through the world with our eyes half closed and our focus divided.

EXERCISE – Take a walk with eyes, ears, nose, and mind wide open. What do you observe? If you were more consciously observant, in what ways might it influence your work life? Family life?

EXERCISE – Sit in a coffee shop or in your company lunchroom with your computer open to a blank screen—so as to appear working but not be distracted. Listen to the conversations around you. What do they tell you about what matters to human beings? How might you apply these insights to the questions you are asking and obstacles you are facing?

Two other experiences in the Studio that we use to practice noticing are tea and coffee tastings—the latter with a chocolate pairing, of course. Sommeliers with well-trained palettes can differentiate not only what country a tea or coffee comes from, but also what side of the mountain it grew on and if it was a good or bad season for rain. The nuances of oaky, fruity, citrusy, earthy, or nutty are not lost on them as they are on most of us. A gift? Maybe. Alongside years of practice. It is amazing how genius develops overnight when years of work have preceded it! Applying the ability to notice to Bridge Building Leadership, we can see that those who have trained themselves to pay attention will observe more than others. They will notice that someone now feels too unsafe to contribute to the conversation, that alliances are going sideways, or that the person sitting on the street corner who you have passed dozens of times is a human being with a story, a family and a future.

REFLECTION – Why is the ability to truly see what is going on important to your life and work? What are you doing to hone your noticing skills?

2. Vision: In the Leadership Studio, each room has different kinds of windows. Some are large and face beautiful vistas, some are small and above eye level—letting in light but preventing us from seeing out—some are built into the corner of the room to cause your eye to follow up the hill behind, and some are low to force our eyes to look down. This design is intentional, meant to train us and remind us to notice that there are various perspectives on the world. As we have said time and again throughout this book, the wise Bridge Building leader is intentional about both increasing their own perspective and acknowledging that there are perspectives very unlike their own. Leaders are constantly framing both current reality (which says where we are) and future vision (where we could be) for others.

Vision is important. It builds our BRAVE. Anna Fels, interviewing young women for a book on women's ambition, discovered that "the liveliness and pleasure with which [they] told their stories often corresponded closely to their level of self-esteem and general sense of well-being."[232] Women who had a dream were more likely to be confident and animated. That is insightful don't you think? If we are growing weary, complacent or discouraged perhaps our vision needs a boost.

Discuss – What are you dreaming that you have not dared to share with anyone yet?

Expanded Perspective:
Three Critical Skills
(cont'd)

"*The real journey of discovery consists not in seeking
new landscapes but having new eyes.*"
Marcel Proust

Personal Reflection – Where might a fresh set of lenses help me to see in ways that would enable me to be a more effective Bridge Building leader? Where do I need to go to get those lenses?

Vision for Bridge Building Leaders includes understanding where the Bridge begins and ends. It asks: How solid is the ground upon which the foundations will be laid? How big a stretch is required? How important is the end result? How worthy of the effort?

3. SELF-DIFFERENTIATION: There are grave dangers inherent in becoming a Bridge Building Leader. Ironically, one of them is taking it too far. Healthy bridge builders are not serving others to make themselves feel better, feel needed, "fix" others, identify with cool people who care about trendy issues, or build a platform for themselves. Similarly, healthy Bridge Building Leaders do not overextend and burn out (how I wish someone had told me that earlier). They are skilled at setting boundaries.

To be able to set healthy, wise and empowering boundaries Bridge Building Leaders must have a strong sense of personal identity. Otherwise, there is a grave danger that we will look to others to define us, listen to public opinion regarding what is worth fighting for, or allow others to become too dependent on us. Differentiated people walk the razor's edge between deep caring and the ability to detach. In fact the Ancient Mothers and Fathers of many faith traditions referred to this as *Loving Detachment*; the ability to deeply care but not become enmeshed. This is a difficult yet necessary calling.

REFLECT – In what areas could you expand your ability to self differentiate in healthy ways?

An expanded perspective involves looking out (at what is around us), looking forward (at what is possible), and looking inward (at what drives and/or draws us). With a growing perspective, additional skills will be required and BRAVE Bridge Building Leaders understand the importance of the life-long learning necessary to build their toolkit.

"To dare is to lose one's footing momentarily. Not to dare is to lose oneself."
Soren Kirkegaard

EXPANDED SKILLSET

As well as developing an expanded perspective, transformational Bridge Building Leaders know they must dare to expand their competencies. Bridge Building is challenging. Those serious about practicing it must master both the basic skills of leadership and the advanced competencies needed for breakthrough, border crossing and sustainability.

Four important skills for Bridge Building Leaders to develop include:

SKILLS FOR BRIDGE BUILDING LEADERS: MOTIVATION

1. MOTIVATION: As Daniel Pink and others have noted, we all experience four basic motivators: Autonomy, Mastery, Belonging, and Purpose. However, each of us has a primary driver. Knowing and managing what motivates us—and others—will help us to be both more effective in the short run and persistent in the long race. It will also help us to know when we are motivated in unhealthy ways that could derail us—or the initiatives we seek to champion.

Autonomy refers to more than just the desire to work alone. It means the need to feel some control over the choice of activities, pace, and outcomes. People with this primary driver resist constraints, micro-management, and having to do things the way everyone else does.

Mastery refers to the desire for constant improvement and learning. People with this motivator will become discouraged if required to do the same task over and over again in the same way. They may appear to be "never satisfied" as indeed they are not, always wanting to grow, develop, create, and re-vamp.

Belonging, as the name suggests, refers to the motivation to be part of something bigger than oneself. People who share this drive value connection and community. They may strongly dislike conflict and find it difficult to work if relationships are not right. Forcing these folks to focus on tasks, or work in a place where they do not feel respected can be demoralizing.

While purpose and meaning are important to many women and men it turns out that a select group value it even more highly than others. They want to know how what they are doing is going to change the world. If the vision does not appeal or apply to them they can easily become discouraged.

The great irony about motivators is that when we have been disappointed or wounded in this area we swing the opposite way. People who are motivated by belonging may exhibit anti-social behaviour if they don't feel respected or that they fit in. Those motivated by mastery may flame out. Those inspired by autonomy may experience learned helplessness if required to follow too many policies and procedures. Perhaps most interesting of all, people driven by the need for purpose may become cynical and skeptical when disillusioned.

Soon after reading and reflecting on these forces I had the chance to test them in a most unexpected setting. I had travelled to the Center for Creative Leadership in North Carolina to participate in a summit. The day we were to travel home, there were huge storms all along the southern and eastern coasts of the US. Managing to make it as far as Charlotte, I became stuck in the airport overnight when the thousands of other travelers whose flights had been cancelled or redirected had taken every hotel room in the city. Walking aimlessly through the airport in the middle of the night, I met a man who loved to chat. Being an introvert, I sought to subtly but firmly set a wide boundary. However, he was determined to talk. Not only did this gentleman love to chat but he also loved conspiracy theories. Eight hours of rants and warnings later, minutes before I was going to board my plane, he repeated for the umpteenth time that he was a skeptic. It was as if I woke up. I told him that I had recently read that people who are the most skeptical are often those who were actually idealistic before disappointment and disillusionment set in. To my great surprise his eyes filled with tears and he began to tell his story. This man, whose name I never learned, had gone to university intending to set the world on fire. He joined and soon led numerous groups protesting war, environmental issues, and supporting other causes. Discovering that the leaders of these protest groups were using the same less-than-honorable techniques as those they were seeking to influence, he quit his associations, dropped out of school, and never protested again. That was forty years ago.

Understanding what motivates us, as well as being able to recognize the seeds of what motivates others—even when it shows up in its shadow side—is a skill that is crucial to Bridge Building Leaders. Without it we will assume that what motivates us will motivate others, ignore the signs of burnout or disillusionment in ourselves and others, and or undermine the effectiveness of our work when our shadow side shows up in unhealthy ways.

SKILLS FOR BRIDGE
BUILDING LEADERS:
SPECIALIZATION

2. SPECIALIZATION: We know we cannot be everything to everyone… and yet we still try. BRAVE Leaders are skilled at culling out all but the most important aspects of their lives and work so as to create a laser focus, knowing they can only build so many bridges at one time. At the same time, however, they stay open to opportunities that appear out of the blue. At the same time, however, they stay open to opportunities that appear out of the blue, that could take the mission further than they ever believed. Any change takes focus and commitment. BRAVE Leaders avoid the temptation of busy-work and scattered approaches.

REFLECT – What are the one to three "key things" you are focused on these days? Are there any bridges that you need to cross? Are there any bridges you need to burn?

"*The hardest thing in life is to know which bridge to cross and which to burn.*"
Scottish Proverb

3. RISK-TAKING: Trustworthy people still make mistakes. As we mentioned when discussing the character trait of sincerity, being trustworthy means owning up to mistakes. This reality actually frees us up to take risks. Bridge Building Leaders understand the importance of taking some calculated risks. In fact it would be difficult to build transformational bridges without doing so from time to time. Pushing ourselves outside our comfort zone enables us to learn new skills and grow in confidence. It also reminds us that even if we fail, it is not as earth shattering as we once thought.

"You gain strength, courage and confidence by every experience in which you really stop to look fear in the face. You are able to say to yourself, 'I have lived through this horror. I can take the next thing that comes along.' You must do the thing you think you cannot do."

Eleanor Roosevelt

DISCUSS – What risk have you been avoiding and why?

PERFECTIONISM IS THE ENEMY OF RISK TAKING. It also kills confidence and divides teams. Yet it is a pervasive problem in girls and women. Listen to the following responses of girls to the question, "What is challenging about being a leader?"

Sarah aged 11, *"I feel that because I am a leader I am supposed to do everything right… that if I do something wrong I would be a terrible leader."*

Madison age 16, *"The hardest thing about being a leader would have to be having everyone looking up to you and trying to be the perfect role-model. You feel the pressure to be perfect, but it is harder than it looks."*

DISCUSS – What role does perfectionism play in your life? Where might it be impeding transformation?

SKILLS FOR BRIDGE
BUILDING LEADERS:
RISK-TAKING

DISCUSS – Where do you find it difficult to experiment? To try before you have all the info or expertise? To stand in front of others before you feel ready to?

Bridge Building Leaders and BRAVE women actually enjoy some failures. Reshma Saujani, founder of *Girls Who Code* found that teaching girls computer coding helped them become more comfortable with risk-taking and failure. To get a code "right" requires multiple experiments and attempts. Coding teachers noted that at the beginning of the program, boys were much more likely to show what they had accomplished and ask about where they were having trouble. Girls would erase vast amounts of work rather than reveal their flaws. By the end of the program all of that had changed.[233]

DISCUSS – Where have you failed recently? How spectacular a fail was it? What would you be doing if you were less afraid of failing?

4. Execution: Many leaders find it difficult to actually execute on what they dream about. Perhaps this is why many potential world-changers never see the changes they can envision. Bridge Building Leaders understand the power of careful planning—who is going to do what, when. They know to measure success based on whether or not they are actually moving toward the vision. They celebrate small wins by accessing low-hanging fruit to build confidence. They practice baby-steps towards progress until enough momentum builds for more significant forward movement. They build strong teams. Any effective team will include visionaries who will reach for the stars, operators who are grounded and those who pull the two together. Bridge Building Leaders build their teams wisely for maximum impact.

Reflect – Do you have the right people on your team to ensure the dreams you are dreaming get off the ground? Do you have a clear plan for execution and can everyone see the link between the plan and the goal? Is authority shared in such a way as to avoid bottlenecks and one-sided thinking?

Exercise – Reflect on how important being equipped is to Bridge Building Leaders. What resources have you gleaned from working through the exercises and tools in this workbook? What other skills and insights do you have that might be helpful in equipping other girls and women? Develop a simple plan for how to pass on what you have learned, starting this week.

Skills for Bridge Building Leaders: Execution

SKILLS FOR BRIDGE
BUILDING LEADERS:
SYSTEMS THINKING

5. SYSTEMS THINKING: Extended families, ecosystems, hospitals, companies, schools, communities, or airports are all examples of dynamic systems with many interdependent parts. In fact, one of my favorite travel stories involves an airport system. On route to the Republic of Georgia we stopped overnight in Istanbul. Arriving early in the evening we took a cab to our hotel—noting it was a fifteen-minute drive—threw our bags into our rooms and went out to explore this dynamic city. Very early the next morning our prearranged cab arrived at the door to return us to the airport for the final leg of the journey. We had given ourselves forty minutes to get back thinking, at such an early hour there would not be much traffic and that would give us time to enjoy an amazing Turkish coffee before boarding. There had been a huge storm over night and the power in our hotel was off. Unbeknownst to us there had been various international conferences held in Istanbul and many delegates were rushing through the dark streets to the airport from all corners of the city.

When we reached the giant round about that serves as the main entrance to the airport the trouble began. Torrential rain, no streetlights, and far more cars than the roundabout could accommodate created the kind of massive traffic jam one normally only sees in movies. People were abandoning their taxis as they crossed eight lanes of traffic pulling massive suitcases in an attempt to make it to their flights on time. Drivers honked and yelled. There were people standing on the roof of their vehicle to try to get a better view of what was happening.

Our driver somehow got us to the outside edge of the round about. With two wheels on the road and two on the surrounding cement embankment; relentlessly honking, swearing and using hand gestures I have never seen before; he somehow got us around the mess in an amazingly short period of time. Getting into the airport was another question. In broken English (much better than my Turkish) he explained he would take us to arrivals since it would be less busy than departures. From there we could make our way through the airport to departures and hopefully still catch our flight. We thanked and tipped him well and started to run.

The already long lineups at check-in were slowed further by the fact that half the power in the building was on and half off. Some conveyors were working. Others were not. Some flights were cancelled due to poor weather in Istanbul or at the flight's destination, many delayed because food trucks or crews could not get to them, some, miraculously, moving on time. Some computers functioned perfectly, others—as evidenced by the angry look on customers' faces and growing number of security guards converging on those lineups—not. Somehow we got checked in and watched our suitcases—filled with teaching supplies and gifts for our hosts—move ever so slowly down the conveyor belt. Literally and metaphorically it was the perfect storm. It was also a classic example of a system gone awry; or, more accurately the convergence of multiple systems.

Discuss – What systems collided in the story above? How did one influence the other?

Any group of people—and certainly any organization with multiple departments or community with various members—is more accurately served by considering it as dynamic system in which changing one piece will invariably change many others. We sometimes call these pieces levers. Imagine a complex design of dominoes standing on end and close enough to each other that one falling creates a—no other way of saying it—domino effect. Bridge Building Leaders understand that simple fixes often lead to unintended outcomes. This is what makes changing our world so challenging. A friend was working in a shack city in South Africa. With the best of intentions she taught a few of the women a cottage industry and watched with delight as this not only enabled them to feed their own children but also hire others and develop a sense of autonomy and dignity… until others in the area learned of the increased wealth, and began plundering their defenseless home. The entrepreneurs now lived in constant fear of their goods being stolen or children put at risk. This kind of unintended consequence is common in families, organizations and nations—even when the best of minds initiate the best of practices.

SKILLS FOR BRIDGE
BUILDING LEADERS:
SYSTEMS THINKING
(CONT'D)

How then are we to proceed?

It turns out that some systems (both natural and human made) are inherently more resilient than others. "A resilient system that has the capacity to rebound from disturbance does this by increasing its diversity and redundancy, by foregoing growth and speed for sustainability, and by engaging in a wide range of small local actions that connect to one another."[234]

DISCUSS – How resilient is the system you are seeking to work within? What wise practices might enable it to become more resilient? How might looking at this issue, opportunity or challenge as a system enable you to think more thoughtfully about it?

Standing back to look at an initiative, department or problem as a system can be very helpful. Sometimes it is necessary to visually represent the complex web of components and their relationship to each other as positive and negative feedback loops. This discipline helps us to identify root causes, unearth assumptions, prevent costly mistakes and develop contingency plans. Bridge Building Leaders understand there is often more than one bridge to be built.

ASK – What levers are at your disposal that may seem like small moves but could have huge positive impact in the ripple effect they cause?

What assumptions are we making? What "A" leads to "B" cause-and-effect seemingly quick fixes might it be important for us to actually avoid?

Who are the people on the ground that can actually help us see this model more clearly?

What opportunity does this open up for us?

BRIDGE BUILDING LEADERS EXPAND THEIR INFLUENCE, using their expanded perspective and skill sets to build diverse teams, partner across borders, and leverage their relationships and platforms. They are strategic and tenacious in the pursuit of the transformation of lives, communities, and systems.

EXPANDED INFLUENCE

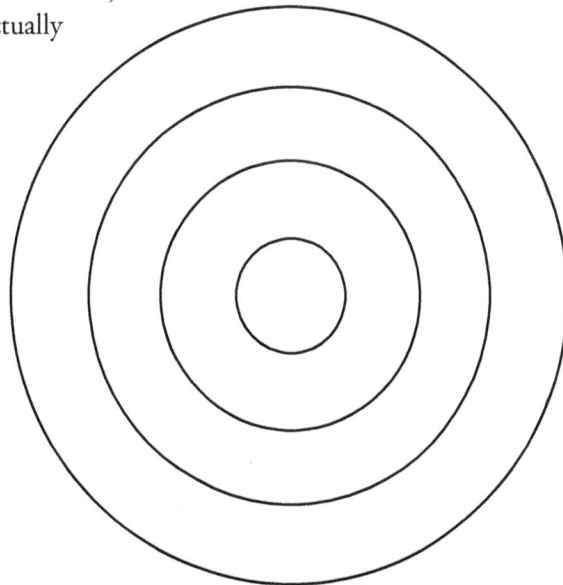

A 2013 study of 64,000 business leaders found that "collaboration, transparency, inclusion, mentoring and innovation" are not only the traits most valued in business but also weapons of transformation.[235] We have discussed how BRAVE Bridge Building Leaders expand our perspectives and skill sets. As we do this we expand our influence—but only as we are intentional about collaboration, inclusion, and mentoring. We will therefore conclude our journey together by returning to the power of vibrant, diverse, co-contributing relationships.

EXERCISE – Using the following graphic, fill in where you have significant to limited influence. For example you may have significant influence over yourself, a bit less over your direct reports and family, less still over friends and colleagues, less still over people you are less connected to etc. This exercise is helpful as it illuminates the fact that we often spend a lot of time stressing over people and projects that we actually can have limited influence over and miss the people and places where we do. In order to expand our influence we have two choices—to go broader or deeper. Wise Bridge Building Leaders understand the power of both. To preach to the masses may be your best strategy some days. Other times, to go deep yourself or with a few others may actually help move the cause much further ahead.

EXPANDED INFLUENCE
(CONT'D)

BRAVE Bridge Building Leaders must be skilled at building trust (the currency of transformational relationships), developing partnerships, and raising those who come after them through mentoring, coaching and developmental delegation, and community decision-making.

1. BUILDING TRUST: Trust takes time to build. It is a byproduct of three R's: Respect + Relationship + Results.

Respect is earned through the consistent demonstration of character, values, and wisdom. Relationships take time to build and involve a genuine commitment to the best interests of the other. Results must match the expectations of the other to build trust.

The three R's interact. To build trust, all three must be consistently demonstrated. No wonder that, without a proven track record, it is difficult to build trust. Even with a history of results, one can quickly lose the trust of those who doubt your commitment to them. While we tend to judge ourselves according to our intentions, we truly do judge others according to their behaviour. We must demonstrate our commitment in ways that align to the way others best can receive it. Wise Bridge Building Leaders are intentional about face time. However, even lots of time together will not compensate for lost respect. The quickest way to lose trust is to say one thing and do another—or say one thing to one person and something else to another. Nowhere is this more pronounced than in those working on behalf of the marginalized and oppressed where trust is a rare and often abused commodity.

PERSONAL REFLECTION – Which of the three R's would others give you the highest ranking on? The lowest? What behaviours might you begin practicing that could make you even more trustworthy without becoming dependent on others approval in your decision-making?

2. TEAM AND PARTNERSHIP BUILDING: Any dream worth dedicating your life to can not normally be achieved alone. However, inviting others in comes at a cost. Things may move slower at first. There may be a watering down of the vision. Differences of opinion arise and time is spent resolving these. More meetings are needed and decisions are not made as quickly. Then, one glorious day you hear someone talking about what *we* do, what *we* believe, what *we* have accomplished and it strikes you that not only could you not have done this alone but that the journey has been sweeter, and stronger with others. In the process you will find that you have grown so much more. The project has gone places you could never have taken it, and will carry on after you are gone.

Speaking like a true Bridge Building leader, civil-rights activist, Jesse Jackson once said, "Leadership has a harder job to do than just choose sides. It must bring sides together."

While most partnerships will be based on trust and shared values, do not discount the value of diversity even here. Tread carefully. This takes great skill and wisdom.

REFLECT – What partnerships would enable your initiative to take off if they could be built with trust and integrity? What potential partners might you have unfairly dismissed?

We will be known forever by the tracks we leave.
Dakota Proverb

EXPANDED INFLUENCE
(CONT'D)

3. MENTORING AND COACHING: Although many of us acknowledge its potential, so few of us have experienced healthy, helpful mentoring or coaching. So many of us are already so overloaded with responsibilities and expectations that adding additional, intentional relationships may seem daunting. I have often felt this way. Yet, with a good coach, my perspective and productivity soars. Investing in women of promise has resulted in me gaining more than they do in both insight and inspiration.

The key is setting realistic boundaries. Like many female leaders you may at times be inundated with requests to mentor. The following guidelines may be helpful.

- When you meet someone with shared interests and chemistry, invite them to meet for coffee to discuss a project or topic of mutual interest. See how it goes. If it goes well commit to two to three more times. It is amazing what can be achieved in four targeted sessions if both parties come prepared with questions, insights, and the names of someone else the other should meet. This approach not only builds confidence through affirming, inviting, informing, and encouraging them,[236] it also helps develop their network and skill set. Perhaps even more importantly it also teaches them how to invest in others ever after.
- When you see someone with potential, find a way to offer them a task in which you can work together. Delegate wisely, such that they can see you both believe in them and will be there for them. Choose a project that will give them both experience and exposure to others who may be helpful to them in the future.
- Our goal is not that they love and need us for the rest of their lives, but rather to help them take a next step and help others do the same. Many mentees will remain as friends or colleagues long after the formal relationship is over. Some will circle back for advice from time to time, but ideally the relationship will have grown into a peer learning one regardless of difference in age or situation.

One other clarification may be helpful here. While coaching and mentoring are in many ways similar they are different in this one important regard. Mentoring involves sharing advice and opening doors for someone so as to expose them to ideas, processes, people or opportunities they would not otherwise have. Coaching involves helping someone access the wisdom, decisions, resources, strengths and potential *they already have* through effective questioning and the assignment of exercises, stretch goals or tasks. Although one is not more important than the other, I find that coaching can be a very effective strategy with women, especially those stuck in stage two[237] who lack confidence in their own knowledge or abilities. It is also important for those who will not have you in their life for long.

Effective mentor-coaches switch back and forth between the two styles seamlessly. However, in my experience, mentoring is easier and we may be tempted to spend too much time there inadvertently training those whom we desire to have wings to become tied to our nest instead.

Discuss – Who in your life acts as a coach for you? A mentor? Are you accessing them frequently enough? Are you coming prepared and gaining as much as you could from your times together?

Who are you intentionally pouring into? Are you being strategic in the way you maximize your time together?

EXPANDED INFLUENCE
(CONT'D)

4. COMMUNITY DECISION-MAKING: While not every decision is best made by the group, some are. This is especially true when one is seeking to build confidence and stand with those who have previously seen themselves as voiceless.

*"A leader is judged not by the length of their reign
but by the decisions they make."*
Klingon Proverb

The egalitarian models of decision-making used by Civil Rights activists, Women's activists, and Occupy Movements grow out of a rich and textured past. As early as 1142 the Haudenosaunee (mentioned earlier in the story of Pauline Johnson) were practicing consensus decision-making. Of the fifty chiefs assembled around an important decision, one was given special status of consensus, using a 75% majority as a rule of thumb.[238] This was represented visually with a beaded Circle Wampum with fifty strands radiating out. One strand was longer than the others, representing the presence of the Peacemaker who brought them together, and his ambassador, the one chosen to fill this role. Over hundreds of years the Great Law presided over Grand Councils teaching that everyone had a right to voice their opinion and that all people affected by a decision had an equal voice.[239]

In some settings these principles still apply. For example, in 2007 Norma General, Elder of the Wolf Clan Cayuga Nation, said, "True consensus is built through talking, listening, and considering different ideas until a new understanding takes place, and the decision makers come to 'one mind' about what to do. Everyone must have a voice. Everyone has their own stories, their own perspectives—gifts they bring to the process that create balance. No one is left out."

Early Quakers and Anabaptists followed a similar method believing that it could be traced to early church practices. However, it is from the Greeks we can perhaps learn the most about the strengths and weaknesses of this approach. The symbol of democracy in Greece was a raised hand. A raised hand meant one equal vote for all. These raised hands normally held a sword, indicating that one was also willing to fight for a decision. Violence aside, this is an insightful concept. In decision-making we are looking not only for agreement but commitment, the willingness to fight for what we have just agreed to.

Of course, democracy and equality in Greek times were only for the select few: white, Greek, male, free citizens. Indeed, "one of the paradoxes of Greece's Golden Age is that while democracy was being born, the rights of women were eroding… restructuring the culture into a masculine-dominated form and strip[ping] women of the rights, both religious and otherwise, that they had enjoyed in the Heroic Age (1600 through 1100 BC)."[240] In one of the most telling of historical distortions of democracy, *heitairai*,[241] "women [who served as highly paid and esteemed prostitutes] of beauty, education, culture, and attraction, out[shone] in every aspect the virtuous wives who were engaged in breeding and rearing the children of the race." They conversed with men on nearly equal terms, rode about freely through the streets of Athens and "enjoyed a measure of honor, freedom and privilege that respectable women could only dream of."[242]

Women in Greece, the "birthplace of democracy," would not be allowed to vote until 1952. Contrast this to the freedom, authority, agency, and respect of women in nearby Egypt, where women were viewed not as property but as someone with whom to share life. Women participated in all forms of societal life, and there were six known female rulers. Equality for *some* does not mean equality. BRAVE Bridge Building Leaders ensure that equality is genuine and inclusive. They also find ways to hear voices before decisions are made.

DISCUSS – What decision-making processes do you have in place and how disciplined and diverse are they?

Transitioning from thinking about skills and mindsets, we conclude with a few final thoughts about transformation.

A kettle boils at 100 degrees Centigrade. At that point there is a change of state and water becomes steam. A transformation occurs. The interesting point here is that it takes 5-7 times more energy to move the temperature up the final tiny bit such that water can become steam. Bridge Building Leaders do not settle for 99 degrees. They understand that transformation does not occur here.

Transformational leadership describes not a set of behaviours but an ongoing process in which "leaders and followers raise one another up to higher levels of morality and motivation."[243] It transcends short term goals focusing on higher level intrinsic needs, ideals and values. True leadership enables positive change in the environment, as well as positive change in the people involved. This is what makes transformational leadership styles so powerful—members of a team experience deep change and growing confidence even as they are working for change in the world around them. Transformational leadership requires courage; resilience and calculate risk-taking; advocacy and action; authentic voice inspired by our values; and an expanded perspective.

In this model of leadership, vision is inspiring. Values are acted upon. Standards are high. Work is purposeful. Relationships are genuine and trusting. There is a shared optimism that change is possible. Respect is high, and responsibility is shared. BRAVE Bridge Building Leaders embody this mindset and practice its principles.

DISCUSS – Where have you observed transformational leadership at work? What did you observe about it? Which components are you most likely to demonstrate? Least likely to demonstrate? How will you intentionally practice these skills?

And so we come to the end of this shared journey. I'd like to offer one final reflection exercise that may help to pull it all together for you. Take your time with this and see where it leads you.

Exercise – Old Story / New Story

Open your journal to a fresh double page. Imagine that the left hand page represents your life up until now—the good, the bad, and the ugly. The centerline represents this moment in time. The right hand page represents everything from this moment forward. Using whatever process is most helpful and whatever medium if most inspiring for you, craft a timeline, collage, list, compilation of symbols, or whatever works for you. Begin to fill the left hand page with the events, relationships, and internal and external messages that have shaped who you are and how you think. Some may be major and others may seem quite small, but if they seem significant to you, include them. Now thoughtfully choose which of these messages, patterns, and priorities you want to carry with you into the future. Consider the insights you have learned from this book. Record these on the right hand page of the journal leaving room to add whatever other experiences, relationships, beliefs, priorities etc. that you want to add. Title the right hand side BRAVE Bridge Building and dare to draw the bridge large enough to fit your values and dreams.

Conclusion

I AM WRITING THIS FINAL CHAPTER FROM VICTORIA, BRITISH COLUMBIA on the West Coast of Canada. The weather has been rainy so today, feeling grumpy, I almost did not go out for a walk. I am so thankful that I did, otherwise I might have missed two serendipitous and meaningful events. The first occurred when, taking the wrong street, I stumbled across Emily Carr's house. Emily was an iconic Canadian painter, environmentalist and activist whom I have long admired. She was a risk-taker, bridge builder and culture shaper, yet her life was far from easy. Emily lived before her time. She did not fit the mold. Few BRAVE Bridge Building Leaders will.

The second gift caused me to laugh aloud with joy. We were touring the Victorian style Legislature Building when I noticed the elaborately carved and painted dug out canoe in the rotunda. Light poured in from windows three stories above. The canoe was carved from a red cedar log—found by the former Lieutenant Governor, the Honorable Steven Point, when walking along Ross Bay Beach. The log's tapered ends suggested that perhaps someone had begun carving it five hundred years before. The Lieutenant Governor and his friend crafted the log into a traditional inland river canoe called a *Shxwtitostel*, meaning "a safe place to cross the river" in Halq'eméylem. The plaque on the wall explained that the name and project represent a bridge between two peoples. This is where our journey began, and today as I type the last words of this book a powerful confirmation and full circle moment occurs. The canoe is a life-long friend of mine as well as a powerful Canadian symbol.[244] Canoes slip through both deep and shallow waters, going places no other boat can go. They take great skill in navigating and sustained energy to propel. They are nimble, changing direction and speed as needed. They enable us to pause and reflect or, as Pauline reminded us, require us to make some ripples to move forward. Yet until today I had never seen a link between canoes and bridges. As a young woman I spent many happy hours in a canoe in Muskoka floating downstream amidst sighing pines and gorgeous granite cliffs. As a grandmother it is still one of my favorite outdoor activities. The canoe is a graceful craft, traditionally a labor of love and skill honed over years of practice. They are vessels for crossing over, for long journeys of discovery and for new beginnings. And they serve as bridges where none have yet been built.

Perhaps you, like I, have lived long enough to see both breakthroughs and set backs on our journey, to be heartened in some seasons and disillusioned and weary in others. I invite you to take the momentum of both and to use them to build the bridge that only you can build. I invite you to choose Bravery. To allow hope to fuel your Resilience whenever you fall or get knocked down. To Advocate and Act wisely and compassionately wherever you can. To cultivate the power of your Voice. To Expand your skills, perspective and influence. To *Be you, bravely*. For only then can we together build the kind of world we want for children seven generations from now.

END NOTES

INTRODUCTION

1. Rich Morin, "The most (and least) culturally diverse countries in the world," Pew Research Center, accessed July 2017, http://www.pewresearch.org/fact-tank/2013/07/18/the-most-and-least-culturally-diverse-countries-in-the-world.
2. John Seaward, *Observations on the Re-building of London Bridge* (London: J. Taylor Architectural Library, 1824), V.
3. Hanna Rosin, "New Data on the Rise of Women," TED Talks 2010.

CHAPTER ONE: THE HIGH COST OF LOW CONFIDENCE

4. Natalia Brzezinski. "Building Our Daughters' Self Esteem By Starting with Our Own," HuffPost (Blogs), June 4, 2010.
5. For the sake of simplicity we will use the words self-esteem, self-efficacy, confidence and bravery interchangeably throughout although I realize they have nuanced differences of meaning.
6. KPMG "KPMG Women's Leadership Study."
7. Wallace Immen, "How they managed to rise to the top," *The Globe and Mail*, Friday, Nov. 13, 2009.
8. See for example Crandall, Stipek, and Hoffman's work on the negative correlation between intelligence and anticipation of success in young women.
9. Avivah Wittenberg-Cox and Alison Maitland, *Why Women Mean Business* (Chichester: Wiley, 2009), 238.
10. Ibid., 237-239
11. Other barriers included stress, fear of speaking in front of others, seeming bossy, and peer pressure. Girl Scout Research Institute, "Change It Up! What Girls Say About Redefining Leadership."
12. Girl Scout Research Institute, "Change It Up! What Girls Say About Redefining Leadership," 2008.
13. Girl Scout Research Institute, "Exploring Girls' Leadership: Research Review."
14. Girl Scout Research Institute, "The State of Girls: Unfinished Business."
15. Ibid.
16. Johnston, Lloyd D. et al, "Monitoring the Future, a Continuing Study of American Youth," Ann Arbor, MI: Inter-university Consortium for Political and Social Research.

17. Adapted from Sue Monk Kidd, *When the Heart Waits: Spiritual Direction for Life's Sacred Questions* (HarperOne, 2016).

18. Canadian Women's Foundation, "The Facts About the Gender Wage Gap in Canada."

19. René Morissette, Garnett Picot and Yuqian Lu, "The evolution of Canadian wages over the last three decades," Statistics Canada, 2011, 11.

20. Sally Helgeson and Julie Johnson, *The Female Vision: Women's Real Power at Work* (Berrett-Koehler, 2010), 11.

21. Lois Joy et al., "The Bottom Line: Corporate Performance and Women's Representation on Boards," Catalyst, October 2007, quoted in Helgeson and Johnson, *The Female Vision*, 23. See also the 2016 Catalyst study "The Bottom Line: Corporate Performance and Women's Representation."

22. Catalyst, "Companies With More Women Board Directors Experience Higher Financial Performance, According to Latest Catalyst Bottom Line Report."

23. Perlberg, Steven, "Study: Companies With Women On The Boards Perform Better," ThinkProgress.

24. Helgeson, Sally and Julie Johnson, *The Female Vision: Women's Real Power at Work,* quoted in Harriet Rubin, "Where Were the Women?" Strategy+Business

25. Helgesen, Ibid., 29.

26. Felice Schwartz, "Management Women and the New Facts of Life," *Harvard Business Review 67,* (1989): 65-76.

27. Helgesen, Ibid., 30. Study undertaken with the National Council for Research on Women

28. Helgesen, Ibid., 31.

29. Linda Tarr-Whelan, *Women Lead the Way* (Berrett-Koehler, 2011), 41-2.

30. Ibid.

31. Alexandra Delis-Abrams, Ph.D. "Your Self Esteem is Up to YOU."

32. Nicholas D. Kristof and Sheryl WuDunn, *Half the Sky: Turning Oppression into Opportunity for Women Worldwide* (New York, NY: Knopf, 2009), xx, xxi.

33. See for example, Opportunity International "Key Focus Areas: Women."

34. Using data compiled by the United Nations and other international agencies in eighty-nine countries, this study conducted by the Center for Partnership Studies, compared measures of the status of women with quality of life measures such as infant mortality, human rights ratings, and percentage of the population with access to health care.

35. Linda Coughlin, Ellen Wingard, and Keith Hollihan, eds., *Enlightened Power: How Women Are Transforming the Practice of Leadership* (San Francisco, CA: Jossey- Bass, 2005), 27.

36. Chandra Mudaliar, "India's Gender Reservation Policy and Women's Emerging Political Leadership at the Grassroots"; quoted in Linda Tarr-Whelan, *Women Lead the Way,* 20-21.

37. Margaret Alva, general secretary of the All India Congress Committee, at Salzburg Global Seminar, September 2006, based on government reports; quoted in Linda Tarr-Whelan, *Women Lead the Way.*

38. Susan Carroll, *The Impact of Women in Public Office* (Bloomington, IN: University Press, 2001), quoted in Linda Tarr-Whelan, *Women Lead the Way*, 21.

39. Linda Tarr-Whelan, *Women Lead the Way*, 4.

40. Ibid, p. 19.

41. Ibid.

42. Ibid.

43. Ibid, xxi.

44. Sally Helgesen, *The Female Advantage* (Doubleday, 1995), 45.

45. Carol Gilligan, *In a Different Voice* (Cambridge: Harvard University Press, 1982), 44-62.

46. See political scientist James MacGregor Burn's work and language on Transformational Leadership (See Bibliography). For an overview of his concepts and a list of further sources, read Langston University's overview https://www.langston.edu/sites/default/files/basic-content-files/TransformationalLeadership.pdf. Accessed July 2017. See also Bernard M. Bass, *Leadership and Performance Beyond Expectations* (Free Press, 1985), and "From Transactional to Transformational Leadership: Learning to Share the Vision."

47. Alice H. Eagly and Linda L Carli, *Through the Labyrinth: The Truth About How Women Become Leaders* (Boston: Harvard Business School Press, 2007), 129. Quoting the results of a 2003 study done by Eagly, Johannesen-Schmidt, and van Engen and substantiated by Antonaskis, Avolio, and Sivasubramaniam, 2003.

48. The 2012 Disney/Pixar Movie that caused a stir when first its writer and Director, Brenda Chapman, was replaced and later her character Merida was remade thinner, tidier and prettier for sale as doll.

49. from 1184-1213.

50. World Economic Forum's Longitudinal, "Gender Gap Index."

51. For example see Leslie Pratch and Jordan Jacobowitz's study "Gender, Motivation, and Coping in the Evaluation of Leadership Effectiveness" or McCormick, Tanguma, and Lopez-Forment's 2002 Study on the Correlation between Self-Efficacy and Leadership from *the Journal of Leadership Education.*

52. See Crandall, Stipek, and Hoffman's work on the negative correlation between intelligence and anticipation of success in young women; quoted in *Women's Ways of Knowing*, Mary Field Belenky et all, 196.

53. Linda Tarr-Whelan, *Women Lead the Way: Your Guide to Stepping Up to Leadership and Changing the World* (San Francisco, CA: Barrett-Koehler, 2009), 56.
54. KPMG "KPMG Women's Leadership Study," 2015, 10.
55. Nicholas D. Kristof and Sheryl WuDunn, *Half the Sky: Turning Oppression into Opportunity for Women Worldwide* (New York, NY: Knopf, 2009), xvii.
56. See "Women's Pathway" in Appendix.

CHAPTER TWO: BUILDING BRAVE LEADERSHIP

57. Girl Scouts of the USA, "Transforming Leadership: Focus on Outcomes of the New Girl Scout Leadership Experience."
58. Girl Scout Research Institute, "Change It Up! What Girls Say About Redefining Leadership."
59. Girl Scout Research Institute, "Exploring Girls' Leadership: Research Review."
60. See, for example John C. Maxwell, *Failing Forward: Turning Mistakes into Stepping Stones for Success.*
61. Findings from the National Study on "Developing Leadership Capacity in College Students," carried out by Dugan and Komives with over 50,000 students from 52 campuses as part of the Multi Institutional Study for Leadership: A Project of National Clearinghouse for Leadership Programs, USA, 2007.
62.Rosabeth Moss Kanter, *Confidence: How Winning Streaks and Losing Streaks Begin and End* (New York: Three Rivers Press, 2006), 8.
63. Ibid.
64. See the seminal work done by psychologist Albert Bandura in the area of self-efficacy.
65. N.E. Betz, and G. Hackett, "Applications of Self-Efficacy Theory to the Career Assessment of Women." *Journal Of Career Assessment* 5, no. 4 (Fall 1997): 383-402.
66. Albert Bandura, "Self-efficacy" In V. S. Ramachaudran (Ed.), *Encyclopedia of Human Behavior* (Vol. 4), (New York: Academic Press, 1994), 71-81.
67. According to Bandura's Social Learning Theory, Ibid.
68. According to Reciprocal Determinism as outlined Albert Bandura, *Social Foundations of Thought and Action: A Social Cognitive Theory* (Englewood Cliffs, NJ: Prentice-Hall, 1986).
69. A. Bandura, *Self-efficacy: The Exercise of Control* (New York, NY: W.H. Freeman, 1997).
70. Ibid.

71. Belenky et al, *Women's Ways of Knowing* (Basic Books, 1997), 193-6.

72. Valerie Stead and Carole Elliott, *Women's Leadership* (Palgrave Macmillan, 2009), 70.

73. Rosie Ward, *Growing Women Leaders* (BRF, 2008), 173.

74. In her TED Talk Sheryl Sandberg refers to a 2003 experiment that found that students considered a successful entrepreneur in a case study more likable when her name was changed to a man's. "The data says clearly, clearly, clearly that success and likability are positively correlated for men and negatively correlated for women." This double bind – having to choose between being liked or successful is a major obstacle to many women.

75. Some First Peoples, for example, are uncomfortable with overt praise.

76. For example, some Extroverts may prefer public affirmation to feel truly encouraged.

77. See work by Gary Chapman on the topic of love languages.

78. Yong Dai, Ph.D., Rebecca F. Nolan, Ph.D., and Qing Zeng, Ph.D., "Self-Esteem of Early Adolescents: A National Survey of 8th Graders," Louisiana State University in Shreveport, Session 1221, 1:00-2:50 PM, August 24, 2001.

79. See for example Cummings and Worley's "Career Stages" (Organizational Development Change, 483), and O'Neil and Bilimora's "Three Phases of the Working Life."

80. Delia Clark, "Running Ahead: Women Who Advance, The Experience of Women Who Advance Through Careers in the Absence of Job development Framework: A Grounded Theory Approach," Masters Thesis prepared for John F. Kennedy University, June 2009, 51.

81. See, for example, Daniel J. Levinson, *The Seasons of a Woman's Life* (New York, NY: Ballantine Books, 1997).

82. According to his studies in the US and similar ones in 35 developed countries around the world, Marcus Buckingham, *Find Your Strongest Life: What the Happiest and Most Successful Women Do Differently* (Nashville, TYN: Thomas Nelson, 2009), 17-26.

83. Ibid.

84. Ibid., 16.

85. Ibid., 89-92.

86. Joanna Barsch, Susie Cranston, and Geoffrey Lewis, *How Remarkable Women Lead: The Breakthrough Model for Work and Life* (Crown Business, 2011), 12.

87. Mary Field Belenky et al., *Women's Ways of Knowing: The Development of Self, Voice and Mind*, 10th ed. (New York, NY: Basic Books, 1997), 45.

88. Susan Stewart, "Men, Women, and Perceptions of Work Environments, Organizational Commitment, and Turnover Intentions," Journal of Business and

Public Affairs 1, no.1 (2007).

89. Sally Helgesen and Julie Johnson, *The Female Vision: Women's Real Power at Work* (Berrett-Koehler, 2010), 61-62. It is interesting that they also valued meeting their own standards for performance over competition or being measured against others.

90. Margaret Heffernan, *How She Does it: How Women Entrepreneurs are Changing the Rules of Business Success* (New York, NY: Viking Adult, 2007), 70-92.

91. See, for example, Ana M. Martinez Alemán, "College women's female friendships: A Longitudinal View," Boston College University Libraries, published in *The Journal of Higher Education*, vol. 81. Nu. 5 (October 2010), 553-582.

92. Ana Martinez Alemán 2000.

93. M. K. Welch-Ross, "A feminist perspective on the development of self-knowledge," in P. H. Miller & E. K. Scholnick (eds.), *Towards a feminist developmental psychology* (New York, NY: Routledge, 2000), quoted in Ana Martinez Alemán, "College women's female friendships: A Longitudinal View," *The Journal of Higher Education,* vol. 81. no. 5 (October 2010), 573.

94. Ana M. Martinez Alemán, "College women's female friendships: A Longitudinal View," Boston College University Libraries, published in *The Journal of Higher Education*, vol. 81. Nu. 5 (October 2010), 565-567.

95. R. Kegan, *The evolving self: Problem and process in human development* (Cambridge, MA: Harvard University Press, 1982).

96. Greene, *Psychological development of girls and women: Rethinking change in time* (New York: Routledge, 2003).

97. Ana M. Martinez Alemán, "College women's female friendships: A Longitudinal View," Boston College University Libraries, published in *The Journal of Higher Education*, vol. 81. Nu. 5, 553-582 (October 2010), 575.

98. See Tom Rath, *Vital Friends: The People You Can't Afford to Live Without* (Gallup, 2006).

99. See UCLA social psychologist Shellet Taylor's work on this, "Biobehavioural Responses to Stress in Females: Tend-and-befriend, not Fight-or-flight," *Psychological Review* 107, no.3 (2000), 411, 429.

100. Joanna Barsch, Susie Cranston, and Geoffrey Lewis. *How Remarkable Women Lead: The Breakthrough Model for Work and Life* (Crown Business, 2011), 125.

101. Howard Zehr, *The Little Book of Restorative Justice* (Good Books, PA, 2002), 19-20.

102. Adrienne Clarkson, *Belonging: The Paradox of Citizenship* (CBC Massey Lectures, 2014), 183-4.

103. Adrienne Clarkson, *Belonging: The Paradox of Citizenship* (CBC Massey

Lectures, 2014), 126.

104. Adrienne Clarkson, *Belonging: The Paradox of Citizenship* (CBC Massey Lectures, 2014), 122.

105. Mandivamba Rukuni, *Leading Afrika* (Penguin Books, 2009), 3.

106. Mandivamba Rukuni, *Leading Afrika* (Penguin Books, 2009), 49.

107. Mandivamba Rukuni, *Leading Afrika* (Penguin Books, 2009), 1, 2.

108. *South African Concise Oxford Dictionary* (Oxford, 2002).

109. Mandivamba Rukuni, *Leading Afrika* (Penguin Books, 2009), 72.

110. Ibid, 67.

111. Ibid, 62.

112. Mandivamba Rukuni, *Leading Afrika* (Penguin Books, 2009), 68-9.

113. J. C. Kennedy, *Leadership and Culture in New Zealand, Commerce Division, Lincoln University*, quoted in "Leadership in Aotearoa New Zealand: A Cross Cultural Study," by Dale Pfeifer, Massey University and Matene Love, Victoria University.

114. Dale Pfeifer and Matene Love, "Leadership in Aotearoa New Zealand: A Cross Cultural Study."

115. James Kerr, *Legacy: 15 Lessons in Leadership, What the All Blacks Can Teach us About the Business of Life* (London: Constable, 2013), 10.

116. See for example, Gill, Amarjit, Stephen Fitzgerald, Smita Bhutani, Harvinder Mand, Suraj Sharma, "The relationship between transformational leadership and employee desire for empowerment," *International Journal of Contemporary Hospitality Management*, vol. 22, Issue 2, 263-273.

117. See for example, Mubarak Hussain Haider, Adnan Riaz, "Role of transformational and transactional leadership with job satisfaction and career satisfaction," *Business and Economic Horizons* 1, 2010, 29-38.

118. Brian M. Howell & Jenell Williams Paris, *Introducing Cultural Anthropology* (Baker Academic, Grand Rapids, MI, 2011), 28.

119. Sandrine Devillard, Sandra Sancier-Sultan, and Charlotte Werner, "Why Gender Diversity at the Top Remains a Challenge," *McKinsey Quarterly*, April 2014.

120. Ibid.

121. Ibid.

122. Ibid.

Chapter Three: Developing Resilience

123. Sheryl Sandberg, TED Talk.

124. Researchers from the University of Pennsylvania studied success—in everyone from students to Navy SEALs—and the consistent trait in those who succeeded in their criteria was resilience; quoted in "Group Mentoring for Girls—Building Confidence by Creating a Community of Support." http://selfesteem.dove.us/Articles/Written/Group-mentoring-for-girls.aspx.

125. Nick Petrie, "Vertical Development—Part 1: Developing Leaders for a Complex World," White Paper: Center for Creative Leadership, accessed July 2017, and, "The How-To of Vertical Leadership Development—Part 2: 30 Experts, 3 Conditions, and 15 Approaches," White Paper: Center for Creative Leadership, accessed July 2017.

126. Ibid.

127. See, for example, Richard J. Davidson, Ph. D., with Sharon Begley, *The Emotional Life of Your Brain.*

128. See Emilia Lahti, *Above and Beyond Perseverance: An Exploration of Sisu*, (Master's Thesis). University of Pennsylvania, and her blog at https://sisulab.com. On Resilience, see also Ann S. Masten, "Ordinary Magic: Lessons from Research on Resilience in Human Development," Education Canada 49, 28-32, and Suniya S. Luthar, Dante Cicchetti, Bronwyn Becker, "The Construct of Resilience: A Critical Evaluation and Guidelines for Future Work," *Child Development* 71, 2000, 543-562.

129. Benson & Saito, 2001; Fertman & Van Linden, 1999; Komives, Owen, Longerbeam, Mainella, & Osteen, 2005; Scales & Leffort, 1999; Sire, Ma & Gambone, 1998; Van Linden & Fertman, 1988, quoted in J. P. Dugan and S. R. Komives, "Developing Leadership Capacity in College Students: Findings from a National Study," A Report from the Multi-Institutional Study of Leadership, College Park, MD: National Clearinghouse for Leadership Programs, 2007.

130. Adrienne Clarkson, *Belonging: The Paradox of Citizenship* (CBC Massey Lectures Series, 2014).

131. Hyon S. Chu, "New Technology Industry Diversity and Inclusion report, 2017," *Culture Amp.*

132. Ibid.

133. Ibid.

134. *6 Ways to Foster Belonging in the Workplace: Taking Diversity & Inclusion to the Next Level*, a Culture Amp eBook, 7.

135. See the BRAVE Bridge Building Girls program™ built around these principles

136. Search Institute, "Developmental Relationships."

137. Higher than divorce, economic or unemployment rates according to Jean Twenge, Professor of Psychology, Search Institute research.

138. Ichiro Kawachi and Lisa F. Berkham, "Social Ties and mental health," *Journal of Urban Health,* vol. 78, number 3, 2001.

139. See, for example, "Open DISC Personality Test," at http://personality-testing.info.

140. See, for example, "Jung Typology Test," at http://http://www.humanmetrics.com.

141. My favourite is found at, "Personal Values Assessment," at http://www.valuescentre.com/pva.

142. See, for example, "VIA Survey," http://www.viacharacter.org.

143. If you are working through this book with others you are already ahead of the pack here and have a perfect group to access for these self-awareness exercises.

144. It is important that they are behaviours they personally have observed, not hearsay or an interpretation of intent.

145. Sara Rimer, "For Girls, It's Be Yourself, and Be Perfect, Too," *NY Times,* April 1, 2007.

146. Mary Wallace, *The Inukshuk Book,* Owl Kids, Toronto, 1999.

147. "Inuksuk (Inukshuk)," in *The Canadian Encyclopedia.*

148. Peter Irniq, Inuit Cultural Activist.

CHAPTER FOUR: ADVOCACY AND ACTION

149. Brian M. Howell & Jenell Williams Paris, *Introducing Cultural Anthropology* (Grand Rapids, MI: Baker Academic, 2011), 78.

150. "People are not as alike as Scientists once thought." *The Tech Museum of Information, Stanford.*

151. Chris Marshall, *The Little Book of Biblical Justice,* Good Books, 2005, 36.

152. John Paul Lederach, *The Little Book of Conflict Transformation* (Good Books, 2003), 20.

153. John Paul Lederach, *The Little Book of Conflict Transformation* (Good Books, 2003), 20-21.

154. "Making Peace: Cape Town 2014," *Exhibition Catalogue.* See also, Paula Newton and Thom Patterson, "The girl in the picture: Kim Phuc's journey from war to forgiveness," CNN.com, 2015.

155. Robert J. House, Paul J. Hanges, Mansour Javidan, Peter W. Dorfman, Vipin Gupta, eds., *Culture, Leadership and Organizations: The Globe Study of 62 Societies* (California: Sage Publications, 2004), 5.

156. Robert J. House, Paul J. Hanges, Mansour Javidan, Peter W. Dorfman, Vipin Gupta, *Culture, Leadership and Organizations: The Globe Study of 62 Societies* (California: Sage Publications, 2004), 14.

157. "Meet Josephine Mandamin (Anishinaabekwe), The 'Water Walker,'" *Indigenous Rising: An Indigenous Environmental Network,* 2014.

158. "Ojibwe Grandmother and Water Walker Josephine Mandamin Honored for Conservation," *Indian Country Today,* March 4, 2016.

159. James Kerr, Legacy: 15 Lessons in Leadership, *What the All Blacks Can Teach us About the Business of Life* (London: Constable, 2013), 5.

160. Richard Pascale, Jerry Sternin, Monique Sternin, *The Power of Positive Deviance: How Unlikely Innovators Solve the World's Toughest Problems* (Boston MA: Harvard Business Press, 2010). And Margaret Wheatley, Deborah Frieze, *Walk Out Walk On: A Learning Journey into Communities Daring to Live the Future Now* (San Francisco, CA: Berrett-Koehler Publishers, Inc., 2011).

161. Richard Pascale, Jerry Sternin, and Monique Sternin, *The Power of Positive Deviance* (Harvard Business Review Press, 2010), 5, 6.

162. Richard Pascale, Jerry Sternin, and Monique Sternin, *The Power of Positive Deviance* (Harvard Business Review Press, 2010), 8.

163. Richard Pascale, Jerry Sternin, and Monique Sternin, *The Power of Positive Deviance* (Harvard Business Review Press, 2010), 10.

164. "Universal Declaration of Human Rights," *United Nations.*

165. "11 Facts About Global Poverty," DoSomething.org.

166. Statistics Canada, reported in "25% of Canada's human trafficking victims are minors: Statistics Canada," *Global News,* 2016.

167. "Our Environment," *The World Counts.*

168. "Endangered Species Statistics," *Statistics Brain.*

169. UN Report on violence against women worldwide, 2015.

170. "Prevention is 60:1 Cost Effective," *Friends Committee on National Legislation Report,* 2011.

CHAPTER FIVE: CULTIVATING VOICE

171. *Herstory Calendar 2015: A Canadian Women's Calendar* (Saskatoon Women's Calendar Collective, 2015), 106.

172. Wallace Immen, "How they managed to rise to the top."

173. Jane Stephens and Stephan Zades, *Mad Dogs, Dreamers and Sages: Growth in the Age of Ideas* (New York, NY: Elounda Press, 2003), 92.

174. See, for example, Tim "Mac" Macartney speaking at the Q1 Global 2010

175. Emphasized in Mikhail Bakhtin's Theory of Dialogue. See Bakhtin, and also the student's guide, "Mikhail Bakhtin: Main Theories, Dialogism, Polyphony, Heteroglossia, Open Interpretation," by Martin Irvine at Georgetown University.

176. Mary Field Belenky et al., *Women's Ways of Knowing: The Development of Self, Voice and Mind,* 10th ed. (New York, NY: Basic Books, 1997), 45.

177. Bruce Chatwin, *The Songlines* (Penguin, 1988).

178. A. Mehrabian, "Differences in the forms of verbal communication as a function of positive and negative affective experience," Unpublished doctoral dissertation, Clark University, 1964. See Mehrabian, A. *Silent Messages: Implicit communication of emotions and attitudes.* Belmont, CA: Wadsworth, 1981.

179. Adapted from Inger Lise Oelrich, *The New Story: Storytelling as a Pathway to Peace* (Troubador Publishing, 2014), 26-27.

180. Rupert Ross, *Dancing With A Ghost, Exploring Aboriginal Reality* (Penguin, 2006), xv.

181. Ibid,16.

182. Inger Lise Oelrich, *The New Story: Storytelling as a Pathway to Peace* (Troubador Publishing, 2014), 2.

183. Ibid, 21-23.

184. Ibid, adapted from 93-94.

185. Clance and Imes 1978: Cross 1968; Macoby and Jacklin 1974; Piliavin 1976; West and Zimmerman 1983, quoted in Belenky, Clinchy, Goldberger, and Tarule *Women's Ways of Knowing: The Development of Self, Voice and Mind* (New York, NY: Basic Books, 1997), 5.

186. Aries 1976; Eakins and Eakins1976; Piliavin 1976; Sadker and Sadker 1982;,1985; Swacker 1976; Thorne 1979, quoted in Belenky, Clinchy, Goldberger, and Tarule *Women's Ways of Knowing: The Development of Self, Voice and Mind* (New York, NY: Basic Books, 1997), 5.

187. Hagen and Kahn 1975; Hall and Sandler 1982; Serbin, O'Leary; Kent and Tonick 1973 as quoted in Belenky, Clinchy, Goldberger, and Tarule *Women's Ways of Knowing: The Development of Self, Voice and Mind* (New York, NY: Basic Books, 1997), 5.

188. Gallese 1985; Kanter 1977; Ruddick and Daniels 1977; Sassen 1980; Treichler and Kramarae 1983, quoted in Belenky, Clinchy, Goldberger, and Tarule *Women's Ways of Knowing: The Development of Self, Voice and Mind* (New York, NY: Basic Books, 1997), 5.

189. Belenky, *Women's Ways of Knowing: The Development of Self, Voice and Mind* (New York, NY: Basic Books, 1997), 5.

190. Ibid., 46.

191. Brown and Gilligan, 1992, quoted in Girl Scout Research Institute, "Exploring Girls' Leadership: Research Review."

192. Jackson, 2005, quoted in Girl Scout Research Institute, "Exploring Girls' Leadership: Research Review."

193. Girl Scout Research Institute, "Exploring Girls' Leadership: Research Review."

194. Joanna Barsch, Susie Cranston, and Geoffrey Lewis. *How Remarkable Women Lead: The Breakthrough Model for Work and Life* (Crown Business, 2011), 197.

195. Ibid., 205.

196. Nancy Beach, *Gifted to Lead: The Art of Leading as a Woman in the Church* (Grand Rapids, MI: Zondervan, 2008), 33.

197. Anna Fels, *Necessary Dreams: Ambition in Women's Changing Lives* (Anchor, 2005), 193.

198. Called "Implicit Voice Theory," the study of beliefs held about ones ability and opportunity to speak up. See, for example, James R. Detert and Amy C. Edmondson.

199. Jennifer Kish-Gephant, James R. Detert, Linda Klebe Trevino, Amy Edmonston, "Silenced by Fear: The nature, sources, and consequences of fear at work," *Research in Organizational Behaviour* 29 (2009), 165.

200. Kerry Patterson, Joseph Grenny, Ron McMillan, and Al Switzler, *Crucial Conversations* (McGraw-Hill, 2002), 71.

201. James Detert, classroom notes, "Speaking Up at Work," Cornell-Queens Executive MBA, Cornell University, The Johnson School, NCCB/MBQC 851: Managing and Leading Organizations, Session 8, Summer 2010, 4.

202. Kish-Gephant et al, "Silenced by Fear: The nature, sources, and consequences of fear at work." *Research in Organizational Behaviour* 29, 2009.

203. Peter G. Northhouse, *Leadership, Theory and Practice* (Thousand Oaks, CA: Sage, 1997), 210.

204. Wittenberg-Cox, *Why Women Mean Business* (Chichester: Wiley, 2009), 240.

205. Heim and Murphy, *In the Company of Women: Indirect Aggression Among Women: Why We Hurt Each Other and How to Stop.* (TarcherPerigee, 2003), 23.

206. Ibid., 29.

207. Rupert Ross, *Dancing with a Ghost: Exploring Aboriginal Reality* (Penguin, 2006), 9-10.

208. Linda Coughlin, Ellen Wingard, Keith Hollihan eds. *Enlightened Power: How Women are Transforming the Practice of Leadership* (San Francisco CA: Jossey-Bass, 2005).

209. Pat Heim and Susan Murphy, *In the Company of Women: Indirect Aggression Among Women: Why We Hurt Each Other and How to Stop* (TarcherPerigee, 2003), 38-39.

210. Ibid., 37.

211. Ibid., 48.
212. Ibid., 49.
213. Carol Anderson and Patricia Shafer, "Deeper Power" in *Enlightened Power,* Linda Coughlin, Ellen Wingard and Keith Hollihan, eds., 55.
214. Ann Oakley, *Gender on Planet Earth,* quoting Hacker 1951, (New York, NY: New Press, 2002),
215. See Desmond, William D. *Philosopher-Kings of Antiquity* (Continuum / Bloomsbury, 2011), and C.D.C. Reeve, *Philosopher-Kings: The Argument of Plato's Republic* (Princeton University Press, 1988). And Plato, *The Republic: the complete and unabridged Jowett translation* (New York: Vintage Books, 1991).
216. Judy Bower, *Jane Eyre's Sisters: How Women Live and Write the Heroine's Story* (Quest Books, 2015), 134.
217. Ibid, 135.
218. Ibid, 13.
219. Ibid, 142.
220. See Janet O. Hagberg, *Real Power: Stages of Personal Power in Organizations,* Revised Edition (Salem, WI: Sheffield Publishing Company, 1994).
221. *Herstory Calendar 2015: A Canadian Women's Calendar* (Saskatoon Women's Calendar Collective, 2015), 24.
222. Judy Bower, *Jane Eyre's Sisters: How Women Live and Write the Heroine's Story* (Quest Books, 2015), 66.
223. Ibid, 68-69.
224. Ibid, 147.
225. Ibid, 154.
226. Katsitsakwas Ellen Gabriel, quoted in *Herstory Calendar 2015: A Canadian Women's Calendar* (Saskatoon Women's Calendar Collective, 2015), 60.
227. The Peacemaker's name means "Two River Currents Flowing Together."
228. *Herstory Calendar 2015: A Canadian Women's Calendar* (Saskatoon Women's Calendar Collective, 2015), 52.

CHAPTER SIX: EXPANDED SKILLS, INFLUENCE, AND PERSPECTIVE

229. James Kerr, *Legacy: 15 Lessons in Leadership: What the All Blacks Can Teach Us About the Business of Life* (Constable & Robinson Ltd., London, 2013).
230. See Carol Dweck, *Mindset: The New Psychology of Success* (Ballantine Books, 2007).
231. See, for example, Ronnie Lessem and Sudhanshu Palsule, *Managing in Four Worlds: From Competition to Co-Creation* (Blackwell Business, 1997), Jennifer J.

Deal and Don W. Prince, *Developing Cultural Adaptability: How to Work Across Differences* (Center for Creative Leadership, 2003), Kai Hammerich & Richard D. Lewis, *Fish Can't See Water: How National Culture can Make or Break Your Corporate Strategy* (Chichester: Wiley, 2013), Geert Hofstede, Gert Jan Hofstede, and Michael Minkov, *Cultures and Organizations: Software of the Mind* (McGraw-Hill, 2010), and David Goddard, "Leading in Four Worlds: Cultural Intelligence as a Critical Success Factor in the World of Work," Pertec, 2012.

232. Anna Fels, *Necessary Dreams: Ambition in Women's Changing Lives* (New York, NY: Pantheon Books, 2004), xvii.

233. See her Ted Talk "Teach girls bravery, not perfection."

234. Margaret Wheatley and Deborah Frieze. *Walk Out Walk On: A Learning Journey into Communities Daring to Live the Future Now*. San Francisco, CA: Berrett-Koehler Publishers, Inc., 2011, 121.

235. John Gerzema and Michael D'Antonio, *The Athena Doctrine* (Jossey-Bass, 2013).

236. See the Model of Confidence Building for Women on page 43.

237. See Janet Hagberg's model of Stages of Power, explained on page 153.

238. For many years the US military has used 70% as the number to aim for in terms of information available and people on board before moving forward.

239. See, for example, Haudenosaunee & Raseron:ni Neighbourhood Association of Brantford, "The Circle Wampum," and Encyclopedia Britannica, "Iroquois Confederacy."

240. Jeannine Davis-Kimball, Ph.D. and Mona Behan, *Warrior Women: An Archaeologist's Search for History's Hidden Heroines* (Warner Books, 2003), 121ff.

241. See George Ryley Scott *The History of Prostitution* (T. Werner Laurie, 1936).

242. Jeannine Davis-Kimball, Ph.D. and Mona Behan, *Warrior Women: An Archaeologist's Search for History's Hidden Heroines* (Warner Books, 2003), 123.

243. James MacGregor Burns, *Leadership* (New York, NY: Harper & Row, 1978), 20.

CONCLUSION

244. Both as an iconic representation of the spirit of exploration and love of nature many Canadians share and as a sad reminder of the way the canoe enabled colonists to explore and then trade and then take.

BIBLIOGRAPHY

An online Bibliography is available at bravewomen.ca. All URL's are accurate as of July 2017.

"11 Facts About Global Poverty," DoSomething.org. https://www.dosomething.org/us/facts/11-facts-about-global-poverty.

Alemán, A. M. M. "College women's female friendships: A Longitudinal View," Boston College University Libraries, published in *The Journal of Higher Education,* vol. 81. Nu. 5. October 2010, 553-582.

Anderson, Carol and Patricia Shafer, "Deeper Power" in *Enlightened Power,* Linda Coughlin, Ellen Wingard and Keith Hollihan, eds., 55.

Bakhtin, Mikhail. *The Dialogic Imagination: Four Essays.* Austin: University of Texas Press, 1992.

Bandura, Albert. *Self-Efficacy: The Exercise of Control.* New York, NY: W.H. Freeman, 1997.

———. *Social Foundations of Thought and Action: A Social Cognitive Theory.* Englewood Cliffs, NJ: Prentice-Hall, 1986.

———. Social Learning Theory. Pearson, 1976.

Barsch, Joanna, Susie Cranston, and Geoffrey Lewis. *How Remarkable Women Lead: The Breakthrough Model for Work and Life.* Crown Business, 2011.

Bass, Bernard M., *Leadership and Performance Beyond Expectations.* Free Press, 1985.

———. "From Transactional to Transformational Leadership: Learning to Share the Vision." http://discoverthought.com/Leadership/References_files/Bass%20leadership%201990.pdf.

Belenky, Mary Field, Blythe McVicker Clinchy, Nancy Rule Goldberger, Jill Mattuck Tarule. *Women's Ways of Knowing: The Development of Self, Voice, and Mind,* 10th ed.. New York, NY: Basic Books, 1997.

Betz, N.E. and G. Hackett. "Applications of Self-Efficacy Theory to the Career Assessment of Women." *Journal of Career Assessment* 5, no. 4, Fall 1997.

Bower, Judy. *Jane Eyre's Sisters: How Women Live and Write the Heroine's Story.* Quest Books, 2015.

Brzezinski, Natalia. "Building Our Daughters' Self Esteem By Starting with Our Own." HuffPost (Blogs). http://www.huffingtonpost.com/natalia-lopatni-uk-brzezinski/building-self-esteem-buil_b_600860.html.

Buckingham, Marcus. *Find Your Strongest Life: What the Happiest and Most Successful Women Do Differently.* Nashville, TYN: Thomas Nelson, 2009.

Burns, James McGregor. *Transforming Leadership: The Pursuit of Happiness.* Atlantic Monthly Press, 2003.

———. Leadership. New York, NY: Harper & Row, 1978.

Bushe, Gervaise R. *Clear Leadership: Sustaining Real Collaboration and Partnership at Work.* Nicholas Brealey, 2010.

Byock, Jesse. "The Icelandic Althing: Dawn of Parliamentary Democracy." In *Heritage and Identity: Shaping the Nations of the North,* ed. J. M. Fladmark, pp 1-18. The Heyerdahl Institute and Robert Gordon University. Donhead St. Mary, Shaftesbury: Donhead, 2002, pp. 1-18. Available for download http://www.viking.ucla.edu/publications/articles/icelandic_all-thing.pdf.

Canadian Women's Foundation. "The Facts About the Gender Wage Gap in Canada." http://www.canadianwomen.org/facts-about-the-gender-wage-gap-in-canada.

Catalyst. "The Bottom Line: Corporate Performance And Women's Representation On Boards." Nancy M. Carter, Lois Joy, Harvey M. Wagner, and Sriram Narayanan, contributors. http://www.catalyst.org/knowledge/bottom-line-corporate-performance-and-womens-representation-boards.

———. "Companies With More Women Board Directors Experience Higher Financial Performance, According to Latest Catalyst Bottom Line Report." http://www.catalyst.org/media/companies-more-women-board-directors-experience-higher-financial-performance-according-latest.

Chapman, Gary. *The 5 Love Languages: The Secret to Love That Lasts.* Northfield Publishing, 2015.

Chapman, Gary, and Paul White. *The 5 Languages of Appreciation in the Workplace.* Northfield Publishing, 2012.

Chatwin, Bruce. *The Songlines.* Penguin, 1988.

Connor, Roger L. J.D. "Strategy and Stance: A Framework for Understanding Public Advocacy." Vanderbilt Project on Public Advocacy. Discussion Paper Series, No. 110501. Vanderbilt University Law School, 2005.

Hyon S. Chu, "New Technology Industry Diversity and Inclusion report, 2017," Culture Amp. http://hello.cultureamp.com/ diversity-and-inclusion?utm_campaign=Blog%20Link%20 Campaigns&utm_source=Blog&utm_medium=Belonging_importance.

Clark, Delia. "Running Ahead: Women Who Advance, The Experience of Women Who Advance Through Careers in the Absence of Job development Framework: A Grounded Theory Approach." Masters Thesis prepared for John F. Kennedy University, June 2009.

Clarkson, Adrienne. *Belonging: The Paradox of Citizenship.* CBC Massey Lectures, 2014.

Coughlin, Linda, Ellen Wingard, and Keith Hollihan, eds., *Enlightened Power: How Women Are Transforming the Practice of Leadership.* San Francisco, CA: Jossey-Bass, 2005.

Culture Amp. *6 Ways to Foster Belonging in the Workplace: Taking Diversity & Inclusion to the Next Level, a Culture Amp eBook.* http://hello.cultureamp. com/6-ways-to-foster-belonging-in-the-workplace.

Cummings, Thomas G. and Christopher G. Worley. *Organizational Development and Change.*

Dai, Yong, Ph.D., Rebecca F. Nolan, Ph.D., and Qing Zeng, Ph.D., "Self-Esteem of Early Adolescents: A National Survey of 8th Graders," Louisiana State University in Shreveport, Session 1221, 1:00-2:50 PM, August 24, 2001.

Davidson, Richard J., Ph.D., with Sharon Begley. *The Emotional Life of Your Brain: How Its Unique Patterns Affect the Way You Think, Feel, and Live—and How You Can Change Them.* New York, NY: Plume (a Penguin Imprint), 2012.

Davis-Kimball, Jeannine, Ph.D. and Mona Behan. *Warrior Women: An Archaeologist's Search for History's Hidden Heroines.* Warner Books, 2003.

Deal, Jennifer J. and Don W. Prince. *Developing Cultural Adaptability: How to Work Across Differences.* Center for Creative Leadership, 2003.

Detert, James, classroom notes. "Speaking Up at Work," Cornell-Queens Executive MBA, Cornell University, The Johnson School, NCCB/MBQC 851: Managing and Leading Organizations, Session 8, Summer 2010.

Delis-Abrams, Alexandra, Ph.D. "Your Self Esteem is Up to YOU." Self Growth: The Online Self Improvement Community. http://www.selfgrowth.com/ articles/Abrams1.html.

Devillard, Sandrine, Sandra Sancier-Sultan, and Charlotte Werner, "Why Gender Diversity at the Top Remains a Challenge." McKinsey Quarterly April 2014. http://www.mckinsey.com/insights/organization/ why_gender_diversity_at_the_top_remains_a_challenge.

Dugan, J. P. and S. R. Komives. "Developing Leadership Capacity in College Students: Findings from a National Study," A Report from the Multi-Institutional Study of Leadership, College Park, MD: National Clearinghouse for Leadership Programs, 2007. https://www.researchgate.net/profile/John_Dugan2/publication/237536892_Developing_Leadership_Capacity_In_College_Students_Findings_From_a_National_Study/links/570fca6a08ae68dc79096a74.pdf.

Dweck, Carol. *Mindset: The New Psychology of Success.* Ballantine Books, 2007.

Eagly, Alice H., and Linda L Carli, *Through the Labyrinth: The Truth About How Women Become Leaders.* Boston: Harvard Business School Press, 2007.

Encyclopedia Britannica, "Iroquois Confederacy," https://www.britannica.com/topic/Iroquois-Confederacy.

"Endangered Species Statistics," *Statistics Brain*, http://www.statisticbrain.com/endangered-species-statistics/.

Fels, Anna. *Necessary Dreams: Ambition in Women's Changing Lives.* Anchor, 2005.

Gerzema, John and Michael D'Antonio. *The Athena Doctrine: How Women (and the Men Who Think Like Them) Will Rule the Future.* Jossey-Bass, 2013.

Gill, Amarjit, Stephen Fitzgerald, Smita Bhutani, Harvinder Mand, Suraj Sharma, "The relationship between transformational leadership and employee desire for empowerment," *International Journal of Contemporary Hospitality Management,* vol. 22, Issue 2, 263-273.

Gilligan, Carol. *In a Different Voice.* Cambridge: Harvard University Press, 1982.

Girl Scout Research Institute. "Change It Up! What Girls Say About Redefining Leadership." (2008) www.girlscouts.org/research/pdf/change_it_up_executive_summary_english.pdf.

———. "Exploring Girls' Leadership: Research Review." www.girlscouts.org/research.

———. "The State of Girls: Unfinished Business." http://www.girlscouts.org/content/dam/girlscouts-gsusa/forms-and-documents/about-girl-scouts/research/sog_full_report.pdf.

Girl Scouts of the USA. "Transforming Leadership: Focus on Outcomes of the New Girl Scout Leadership Experience." http://www.girlscouts.org/content/dam/girlscouts-gsusa/forms-and-documents/about-girl-scouts/research/transforming_leadership.pdf.

Greene, S. *Psychological development of girls and women: Rethinking change in time.* New York: Routledge, 2003.

Gregorovich, Andrew. "World War II in Ukraine: The Ukrainian Experience in World War II With a Brief Survey of Ukraine's Population Loss of 10 Million." InfoUkes: An Information Resource about Ukraine and Ukrainians. http://www.infoukes.com/history/ww2.

Goddard, David. "Leading in Four Worlds: Cultural Intelligence as a Critical Success Factor in the World of Work," Pertec, 2012. http://www.pertec.fi/blogentry/44.

Haider, Mubarak Hussain, Adnan Riaz, "Role of transformational and transactional leadership with job satisfaction and career satisfaction," *Business and Economic Horizons* 1, 2010, 29-38.

Hagberg, Janet O. *Real Power: Stages of Personal Power in Organizations.* Revised Edition. Salem, WI: Sheffield Publishing Company, 1994.

Hammerich, Kai & Richard D. Lewis. *Fish Can't See Water: How National Culture can Make or Break Your Corporate Strategy.* Chichester: Wiley, 2013.

Haudenosaunee & Raseron:ni Neighbourhood Association of Brantford. "The Circle Wampum." http://hrnabrantford.com/resources/wampum/the-circle-wampum/.

Heffernan, Margaret. *How She Does it: How Women Entrepreneurs are Changing the Rules of Business Success.* New York, NY: Viking Adult, 2007.

Heim, Pat, Susan Murphy. *In the Company of Women: Indirect Aggression Among Women: Why We Hurt Each Other and How to Stop.* TarcherPerigee, 2003.

Helgesen, Sally. *The Female Advantage: Women's Ways of Leadership.* Doubleday Currency, 1995.

Helgesen, Sally and Julie Johnson, *The Female Vision: Women's Real Power at Work.* Berrett-Koehler, 2010.

———. *The Female Vision: Women's Real Power at Work.* Quoted in Harriet Rubin, "Where Were the Women?" Strategy+Business. https://www.strategy-business.com/article/ac00015?gko=a7c05.

Hofstede, Geert, Gert Jan Hofstede, and Michael Minkov, *Cultures and Organizations: Software of the Mind* (McGraw-Hill, 2010),

House, Robert J., Paul J. Hanges, Mansour Javidan, Peter W. Dorfman, Vipin Gupta, eds. *Culture, Leadership, and Organizations: The Globe Study of 62 Societies.* California: Sage Publications, 2004.

Howell, Brian M. & Jenell Williams Paris, *Introducing Cultural Anthropology. Baker Academic,* Grand Rapids, MI, 2011.

Immen, Wallace. "How they managed to rise to the top." The Globe and Mail. Friday, Nov. 13, 2009. http://www.theglobeandmail.com/report-on-business/how-they-managed-to-rise-to-the-top/article1361762/.

"Inuksuk (Inukshuk)." In *The Canadian Encyclopedia.* http://www.thecanadianencyclopedia.ca/en/article/inuksuk-inukshuk/.

Irvine, Martin. "Mikhail Bakhtin: Main Theories, Dialogism, Polyphony, Heteroglossia, Open Interpretation." A Student's Guide, Georgetown University.

http://faculty.georgetown.edu/irvinem/theory/Bakhtin-MainTheory.html.

Johnston, Lloyd D., Jerald G. Bachman, Patrick M. O'Malley, and John Schulenberg. "Monitoring the Future: A Continuing Study of American Youth (8th- and 10th-Grade Surveys)." ICPSR02350-v2. Ann Arbor, MI: Inter-university Consortium for Political and Social Research [distributor]. https://doi.org/10.3886/ICPSR02350.v2.c.

Katsitsakwas Ellen Gabriel, quoted in *Herstory Calendar 2015: A Canadian Women's Calendar.* Saskatoon Women's Calendar Collective, 2015.

Kawachi, Ichiro, and Lisa F. Berkham, "Social Ties and mental health," *Journal of Urban Health*, vol. 78, number 3, 2001.

Kegan, R. *The evolving self: Problem and process in human development.* Cambridge, MA: Harvard University Press, 1982.

Kennedy, J. C. *Leadership and culture in New Zealand.* Commerce Division, Lincoln University. Lincoln, NZ, 2000.

Kerr, James. *Legacy: 15 Lessons in Leadership, What the All Blacks Can Teach us About the Business of Life.* London: Constable, 2013.

Kidd, Sue Monk. *When the Heart Waits: Spiritual Direction for Life's Sacred Questions.* HarperOne, 2016.

Kish-Gephant, Jennifer, James R. Detert, Linda Klebe Trevino, Amy Edmonston. "Silenced by Fear: The nature, sources, and consequences of fear at work." Research in Organizational Behaviour 29, 2009.

KPMG. "KPMG Women's Leadership Study." 2015. https://womens-leadership.kpmg.us/content/dam/kpmg-womens-leadership-golf/womensleadershippressrelease

Kristof, Nicholas D., and Sheryl WuDunn. *Half the Sky: Turning Oppression into Opportunity for Women Worldwide.* New York, NY: Knopf, 2009.

Lahti, Emilia. *Above and Beyond Perseverance: An Exploration of Sisu.* (Master's Thesis). Pennsylvania University, 2013.

Lederach, John Paul. *The Little Book of Conflict Transformation.* Good Books, 2003.

Lessem, Ronnie and Sudhanshu Palsule. *Managing in Four Worlds: From Competition to Co-Creation.* Blackwell Business, 1997.

Levinson, Daniel J. *The Seasons of a Woman's Life.* New York, NY: Ballantine Books, 1997.

Luthar, Suniya S., Dante Cicchetti, Bronwyn Becker, "The Construct of Resilience: A Critical Evaluation and Guidelines for Future Work," Child Development 71, 2000, 543-562.

"Making Peace: Cape Town 2014." Exhibition Catalogue. https://issuu.com/realexpo/docs/makingpeace_expo_light.

Marshall, Chris. *The Little Book of Biblical Justice.* Good Books, 2005.

Masten, Ann S. "Ordinary Magic: Lessons from Research on Resilience in Human Development," Education Canada 49, 28-32.

———. *Ordinary Magic: Resilience in Development.* The Guilford Press, 2014.

McCormick, Michael J., Jesus Tanguma, and Anita Sohn Lopez-Forment. "Extending Self-Efficacy Theory to Leadership: A Review and Empirical Test." Journal of Leadership Education, Vol. 1, Issue 2, Winter 2002. http://www.leadershipeducators.org/Resources/Documents/jole/2002_winter/JOLE_1_2_McCormick_Tanguma_Lopez-Forment.pdf.

"Meet Josephine Mandamin (Anishinaabekwe), The 'Water Walker.'" *Indigenous Rising: An Indigenous Environmental Network,* 2014. http://indigenousrising.org/josephine-mandamin.

Mehrabian, A. *Silent Messages: Implicit communication of emotions and attitudes.* Belmont, CA: Wadsworth, 1981. Excerpt available http://www.kaaj.com/psych/smorder.html.

Morin, Rich. "The most (and least) culturally diverse countries in the world." Pew Research Center. http://www.pewresearch.org/fact-tank/2013/07/18/the-most-and-least-culturally-diverse-countries-in-the-world. Based on a study by Erkan Goren. "Economic Effects of Domestic ad Neighboring Countries' Cultural Diversity." Center for Transnational Studies, University of Bremen. Working Paper No. 16/2013.

Morissette, René, Garnett Picot, and Yuqian Lu. "The evolution of Canadian wages over the last three decades." Statistics Canada 2011. http://www.statcan.gc.ca/pub/11f0019m/11f0019m2013347-eng.pdf.

Moss Kanter, Rosabeth. Confidence: How Winning Streaks and Losing Streaks Begin and End. New York, NY: Three Rivers Press, 2006.

Newton, Paula and Thom Patterson, "The girl in the picture: Kim Phuc's journey from war to forgiveness," CNN.com, 2015. http://www.cnn.com/2015/06/22/world/kim-phuc-where-is-she-now/index.html.

Northouse, Peter G. *Leadership: Theory and Practice.* Thousand Oaks, CA: Sage, 1997.

Oakley, Ann. *Gender on Planet Earth.* Wiley, 2002.

Oelrich, Inger Lise. *The New Story: Storytelling as a Pathway to Peace.* Troubador Publishing, 2014.

Opportunity International. "Key Focus Areas: Women." http://opportunity.org/what-we-do/key-focus-areas/women.

"Ojibwe Grandmother and Water Walker Josephine Mandamin Honored for Conservation," *Indian Country Today,* March 4, 2016. https://indiancountrymedianetwork.com/news/environment/ojibwe-grandmother-and-water-walker-josephine-mandamin-honored-for-conservation/.

"Our Environment," The World Counts, http://www.theworldcounts.com/
themes/our_environment.

Pascale, Richard, Jerry Sternin, and Monique Sternin, *The Power of Positive Deviance: How Unlikely Innovators Solve the World's Toughest Problems,* Harvard Business Press, Boston MA, 2010.

Perlberg, Steven. "Study: Companies With Women On The Boards Perform Better." ThinkProgress. https://thinkprogress.org/study-companies-with-women-on-their-boards-perform-better-928cb3a72698.

Petrie, Nick. "Vertical Development—Part 1: Developing Leaders for a Complex World." White Paper: Center for Creative Leadership. https://www.ccl.org/wp-content/uploads/2015/04/VerticalLeadersPart1.pdf.

———. "The How-To of Vertical Leadership Development—Part 2: 30 Experts, 3 Conditions, and 15 Approaches." White Paper: Center for Creative Leadership. http://www.ccl.org/wp-content/uploads/2015/04/vertical-LeadersPart2.pdf.

Pfeifer, Dale, and Matene Love. "Leadership in Aotearoa New Zealand: A Cross Cultural Study." *Prism Journal.* http://www.prismjournal.org/fileadmin/Praxis/Files/Journal_Files/Pfeifer_Love.pdf.

Plato. *The Republic: the complete and unabridged Jowett translation.* New York: Vintage Books, 1991.

Pratch, Leslie, and Jordon Jacobowitz. "Gender, motivation, and coping in the evaluation of leadership effectiveness." *Consulting Psychology Journal: Practice and Research.* Vol. 48, 1996, 203-220.

"Prevention is 60:1 Cost Effective," Friends Committee on National Legislation report, 2011. http://www.olympiafor.org/prevention_60_1_cost_effective.pdf.

Ramachaurdran, V.S., ed. *Encyclopedia of Human Behavior.* vol. 4. New York: Academic Press, 1994.

Rath, Tom. *Vital Friends: The People You Can't Afford to Live Without.* Gallup, 2006.

Reeve, C.D.C. *Philosopher-Kings: The Argument of Plato's Republic,* Princeton University Press, 1988.

Rimer, Sara. "For Girls, It's Be Yourself, and Be Perfect, Too." *NY Times,* April 1, 2007. http://www.nytimes.com/2007/04/01/education/01girls.html.

Rosin, Hanna. "New Data on the Rise of Women." TED Talks 2010. TED video. https://www.ted.com/talks/hanna_rosin_new_data_on_the_rise_of_women.

Ross, Rupert. *Dancing With A Ghost, Exploring Aboriginal Reality.* Penguin, 2006.

Rukuni, Mandivamba. *Leading Afrika.* Penguin Books, 2009.

Schwartz, Felice. "Management Women and the New Facts of Life," Harvard Business Review 67, (1989).

Search Institute, "Developmental Relationships." http://www.search-institute.org/research/developmental-relationships.

Seaward, John. *Observations on the Re-building of London Bridge.* London: J. Taylor Architectural Library, 1824.

Scott, George Ryley. *The History of Prostitution* (T. Werner Laurie, 1936).

Sellers, Patricia. "Power: Do women really want it? That's the surprising question more of them are asking when they ponder top jobs in business, academica, and government." Fortune Magazine, October 13, 2003. http://archive.fortune.com/magazines/fortune/fortune_archive/2003/10/13/350932/index.htm.

Snow, Edgar. *The Pattern of Soviet Power.* New York: Random House, 1945.

South African Concise Oxford Dictionary. Oxford, 2002.

Saujani, Reshma. "Teach girls bravery, not perfection." TED Talk. https://www.ted.com/talks/reshma_saujani_teach_girls_BRAVEry_not_perfection?utm_source=tedcomshare&utm_medium=referral&utm_campaign=tedspread.

Statistics Canada research, reported in "25% of Canada's human trafficking victims are minors: Statistics Canada," Global News, http://globalnews.ca/news/2819281/25-of-canadas-human-trafficking-victims-are-minors-statistics-canada/.

Stewart, Susan. "Men, Women, and Perceptions of Work Environments, Organizational Commitment, and Turnover Intentions," *Journal of Business and Public Affairs* 1, no.1, 2007.

Stead, Valerie, and Carol Elliott. *Women's Leadership.* Palgrave Macmillan, 2009.

Stephens, Jane and Stephan Zades. *Mad Dogs, Dreamers and Sages: Growth in the Age of Ideas.* New York, NY: Elounda Press, 2003.

Tarr-Whelan, Linda. *Women Lead the Way: Your Guide to Stepping Up to Leadership and Changing the World.* Berrett-Koehler, 2011.

Taylor, Shelley E., Laura Cousino Klein, Brian P. Lewis, Tara L. Gruenewald, Regan A. R. Gurung, and John A. Updegraff. "Biobehavioural Responses to Stress in Females: Tend-and-befriend, not Fight-or-flight," Psychological Review 107, no. 3, 411-429. https://scholar.harvard.edu/marianabockarova/files/tend-and-befriend.pdf.

The Tech Museum of Innovation. "People are not as alike as scientists once thought." http://genetics.thetech.org/original_news/news38.

United Nations, "Universal Declaration of Human Rights." http://www.un.org/

en/universal-declaration-human-rights/index.html.

Wallace, Mary. *The Inukshuk Book,* Owl Kids, Toronto, 1999.

Ward, Rosie. *Growing Women Leaders: Nurturing Women's Leadership in the Church.* BRF, 2008.

Desmond, William D. *Philosopher-Kings of Antiquity.* Continuum / Bloomsbury, 2011.

Wittenberg-Cox, Avivah, and Alison Maitland. *Why Women Mean Business.* Chichester: Wiley, 2009.

Wheatley, Margaret and Deborah Frieze. *Walk Out Walk On: A Learning Journey into Communities Daring to Live the Future Now.* San Francisco, CA: Berrett-Koehler Publishers, Inc., 2011.

Yankah, Kwesi. "The Akan Trickster Cycle: Myth or Folktale?" Trinidad: University of the West Indies, 1983. https://scholarworks.iu.edu/dspace/bitstream/handle/2022/125/Akan_Yankah.pdf?sequence=1.

Zehr, Howard. *The Little Book of Restorative Justice.* Good Books, 2002.

RESOURCES:

Center for Partnership Studies
https://centerforpartnership.org/

Girl Scout Research Institute: Complete List of Reports
http://www.girlscouts.org/en/about-girl-scouts/research/publications.html

United Nations Commission on the Status of Women
http://www.unwomen.org/en/csw

World Economic Forum's longitudinal Gender Gap Index (2015)
https://www.weforum.org/reports/global-gender-gap-report-2015

www.ingramcontent.com/pod-product-compliance
Lightning Source LLC
Chambersburg PA
CBHW061955090426
42811CB00006B/944